For Renée

Best wishes

1992

Janner on Presentation

About the Author

The Hon. Dr Greville Janner QC is Labour MP for Leicester West. A member of the Parliamentary Select Committee on Employment and on Procedure, he is Chairman of the All Party Safety Group.

Dr Janner is President of the Commonwealth Jewish Council and a former President of the Board of Deputies of British Jews. He is married with three children. He speaks eight languages and has made a massive array and variety of speeches and presentations in most parts of the world – from the United States to Australia and from the Far East and Eastern Europe to Egypt and Israel.

Dr Janner, who is a former President of the Cambridge Union, is the only MP who is also a member of the Magic Circle. He is Chairman of Effective Presentational Skills Ltd, a consultancy providing training for all aspects of presentation.

JANNER ON PRESENTATION

An essential guide to the theory, tricks and techniques of business presentation

Greville Janner

BUSINESS BOOKS

Copyright © Greville Janner 1989

First published in Great Britain by
Business Books Limited
An Imprint of Century Hutchinson Limited
62–65 Chandos Place, London WC2N 4NW

Century Hutchinson Australia (Pty) Limited
89–91 Albion Street, Surry Hills,
New South Wales 2010, Australia

Century Hutchinson New Zealand Limited
PO Box 40–086, 32–34 View Road, Glenfield,
Auckland 10, New Zealand

Century Hutchinson South Africa (Pty) Limited
PO Box 337, Bergvlei 2012, South Africa

British Library Cataloguing in Publication Data
Janner, Greville, 1928–

    Janner on presentation.
    1. Oral communication – Manuals
    I. Title
    808.5

    ISBN 0–09–174045–2
    ISBN 0–09–174040–1 pbk

For details of Greville Janner's public courses, in-company training programmes and consultancy services, contact Paul Secher, LLB, Effective Presentational Skills Ltd., 8 Balfour Place, London W1. Tel: 01–408 2063. FAX: 01–408 2079.

For
Caroline and Daniel
with love and pride
and for Isobel
and welcome to
Esther

Contents

PART III—ON YOUR FEET – AND ON PAPER

PART IV—IN THE CHAIR

PART V—PRESENTING TO SELL

PART VI—TECHNIQUES AND TEAMS

Contents

Introduction

Benjamin Disraeli was once asked how he chose his reading. 'When I want to read a book,' he replied, 'I write one!' When searching for a book to give to executives and professionals to whom my colleagues and I teach presentational skills, I found none, so I wrote one – and I hope that it will bring you pleasure to read and profit to use.

This book is for all those who have to make presentations – who find themselves planted on platforms, before microphones, forced onto radio or television; who sell, before groups of prospective clients or customers, or 'close up' ; who 'pitch' (by whatever name) for orders or for work; who must enthuse or rally their own colleagues or managers, their sales force, or their workforce.

Here, then, is how to make the best of yourself or your case, on your feet or on paper; by telephone or at a press conference; when using photographers, writing letters or composing brochures; using visual aids, presenting yourself for interview for a job or for promotion – or presenting your company's case in a promotion or in self-defence.

Whether you are beguiling a potential client or customer at a dinner, on a golf course or on an aircraft, or projecting the image of your company or corporation at a business lunch or company meeting; whether you are surviving in the media, making business presentations, or selling by mail or telephone – you must study the skills of presentation or risk failure.

Whatever the presentational skill you need, this book aims to provide it – in a way that is readable, practical, and helpful. At best, it should give you enjoyment; at worst, it will provide some lessons learned from my own decades of vividly varied experience.

You may never have to appear before a Parliamentary or Select Committee, or give evidence in court, or address an audience out of doors, or speak through an interpreter. But if you do, this book should help you. Certainly you will need to present before someone – in person, in writing, on film, radio or TV. You feel nervous before an audience? Good. So do all fine presenters. Nervous tension gets the adrenalin flowing. I shall tell you how to harness your nerves; how to *appear*, and then how to *become*, confident.

With a combination of good luck, judicious practice and training, and the adaptation of these practical rules, your task should be much easier, your nervousness less and – with a touch of that good fortune without which no presentation can be fruitful – your success, your influence and your pleasure vastly increased. This book is written to increase whatever may be your business or your pleasure. It is designed to show you how to appear and how to become professional in your presentations.

Two companion volumes to this book – my *Complete Speechmaker and Compendium of Retellable Tales* and *Complete Letterwriter* – cover their particular areas in far greater detail than is given to them here. If you require precedents for your speeches, you will find many in my *Complete Speechmaker* – along with my favourite 'Retellable Tales', many of which you may conveniently slot into your presentations. Sample parts of letters are in my *Complete Letterwriter*, and specific employment letters in our looseleaf service, *Janner's Employment Letters* (Business & Legal Publications Ltd).

This book surveys the entire area of presentation – starting with what are commonly called 'presentations' – to actual or potential customers or clients. I then cover specific techniques for the whole range of presentation, from radio and TV to press and public.

GREVILLE JANNER
London, 1989

Acknowledgments

I am very grateful to my colleagues and partners in JS Associates, who not only join with me in teaching presentational skills, but who have helped me so much in the creation of this book. To Paul Secher, to Robert Lightfoot, and to my daughter, Laura Janner, MA (Cantab), my special thanks.

To Peter Crankshaw, David Roth, Lewis Rudd and Lawrie Simpkin – thank you for your suggestions and reassurance on chapters dealing with radio, visual aids, TV and the press respectively. And to those great caricaturists, Ranan Lurie, Ralph Sallon and Glan Williams, for their marvellous representation of me, through their eyes and pens.

My thanks, too, to the delegates and trainees – from mighty executives to new arrivals – whose real and practical problems have provided the raw material for this work. They will recognise themselves in its pages and I hope that its chapters will be of use – to them as well as to their successors.

PART I

General principles of presentation

1 Self-Presentation

The higher your head appears above the crowd, the more tempting it becomes as a target. The mightier your success, the greater your need to present yourself with distinction. Your image becomes that of your company, your organisation, or your viewpoint.

Skills of presentation are not inborn or inherited. You may be trained and taught in the arts of, say, computer technology, accountancy or engineering. So why not spare the time to take a course in presentation?

Each Wednesday, the Parliamentary Select Committee on Employment sits and takes evidence. We watch with incredulity as people with great power make the worst of their opportunities. Some simply dry up under probing examination. Others ramble on, to the irritation of their questioners – not least those on their own side, who are trying to help them.

There is, of course, a technique for dealing with select committees – just as there is with, for instance, presentation to potential clients or customers, or a pep talk to your sales team, or a confrontation on radio or TV or with the Press. I asked a Conservative trade unionist why his basically traditional and right-wing colleagues consistently elect a well known left-winger as their general secretary. 'Because he's a first-class hit man,' came the answer. 'He knows how to negotiate. He can present our case, and he does a good job for us.'

A statesman once remarked that in a democratic country it is an honour to be in Opposition, but it is the only honour which no politician ever seeks. If politicians are out of office, they may still be in Parliament, in harness, and in business. If executives are out of office, they will also be out of work, unemployed, early retired, or redundant. The higher up you get, the fewer the reasonable alternative jobs. Even if you get that untaxed golden handshake, how long will it last you? And will you not be (literally) bored to death?

One way to achieve or to keep high office is, of course, to perform satisfactorily and to achieve profitable results. But it is perfectly possible to be successful and to appear a failure – conversely, you may even cover up your defects with a veneer of successful self-presentation. It is not only politicians who fool at least some of their

3

public some of the time. Some even manage to fool a majority of them enough of the time to win elections.

Ask yourself, do *you* know how to handle a meeting, a speaker or a chairman? If your company achieves distinction – by abnormal success or failure – could you cope with the media? Do your colleagues present an image of which they, or the company, can be proud? Do you, or they, know how to handle hostile questioning?

If you address a gathering of influential people – some of them actual or potential customers or clients – do you do justice to yourself or your case? Do you know how to make a gracious introduction, to present an appropriate toast, to give a vote of thanks or to accept one?

The boffin must sometimes move out of the laboratory, and the accountant from the office, and the scientist from the drawing board. They are forced into battle with overseas competitors who often have a far more practical, intelligent, sensible and structured approach to presentation – formal or informal, public or private – than our old-fashioned world of the public school and the ancient university, where the learning of presentational skills bears the taint of the ill-bred. The UK is not only losing trade to overseas competition because foreigners may produce goods or services better and cheaper than we do. Their products and services may be inferior to ours, or more costly, but they sell because they are professionally marketed.

Test this theory when you next spend an hour in front of television. Look out for the exceptions. Consider, for instance, why one distinguished scientist succeeds as a captain of industry, while others of equal distinction are lamentable failures. Look at the brilliant executives whom the media turn into mediocrities. Intelligence and industrial or commercial skills cannot save them. Coaching, training and even careful preparation might have done.

I once spent a morning with a distinguished ambassador, engaged in highly controversial negotiations on Britain's behalf. He knew that after his set speech to the particular United Nations organisation, he would be grilled by the Press. As a preliminary, he submitted to a half hour's fusillade from his own senior staff. 'Suppose they ask you, Ambassador, why you did this?' asked one, 'What's your answer?' Or, 'I think that the most dangerous line of questioning will be . . .'

I was reminded of the client whom I once interviewed in a cell at the Old Bailey before he came up for trial on a fraud charge. He had free legal aid and I was his (then very junior) counsel. 'What do you think they're going to ask me?' he enquired, very sensibly.

'I think that the most difficult question that you will have to answer is . . .' And I told him.

'So what's the answer to it, then?' he demanded.

'*You'll* have to answer that one. *You* are giving the evidence. I can suggest questions, but I cannot tell you the answers.'

'You won't?' he protested. 'Then what am I *not* paying you for?'

When preparing for other presentational confrontations, your allies can help you with both questions and answers. Ambassadors and others get questioned and interrogated by those who brief them. Every Prime Minister spends precious hours preparing for the twice-weekly, 15-minute Prime Minister's Question Time. 'What is he likely to ask?' 'What do we answer?' 'What are the facts?' Even those impromptu darts of ministerial wit are sometimes not worth the paper they are written on.

So if preparation and training are good enough for Prime Ministers and ambassadors, why are they ignored by industrial and commercial executives and managers forced to use extraordinary skills? Whatever the purpose of your presentation, failure to prepare for it is plain stupid. Leave that mistake to others.

While techniques vary between, for instance, individual and team, oral and written presentations, many of the basic rules are either identical or adaptable from one medium to another. So while you consider some of the rules as they apply to presentations generally, apply them equally, or as appropriate, when you are presenting on your feet or on paper, on radio or TV.

2   Education, training and style

Style and commercial success are synonymous. The common concept that style will suffice without taught techniques is arrogant and ridiculous. So is the converse – the chip-on-the-shoulder, foot-in-the-mouth inferiority complex approach to public speaking or presentation in any form.

I invited a tycoon to address a private dinner. 'Sorry,' he replied, curtly. 'Nice of you to ask. You and your friends in Parliament do the speaking. I do the work!' What he really meant was: 'I'm afraid of opening my mouth when I'm on my feet in case I make a fool of myself.'

Another told me: 'I came up the hard way. I leave speeches to you fellows with the education.' Education does no one much harm and many top people who missed it in their youth are not ashamed to learn, when their money can buy them time and tuition. Presenting yourself to the public does take courage and is certainly an acquired skill. But if you have that intangible, inexplicable magic – that style of your own – you should not fear its public display.

If the speech or presentation is worth your while to make, it is also worth your own time to prepare. Remember one of Churchill's dicta: 'If I have to make a two-hour speech,' he rumbled, 'I may spend ten minutes in preparation. If it is a ten minute speech, then it could take me two hours.'

The presenter with style is as brief as impact and message permit. There is no reason why executives who are blunt, direct and lucid in conversation should allow their speech to deteriorate into long-winded and indirect blather, the moment they climb to their feet.

Just as there is no single successful style in business – or, for that matter, in anything – so presenters who seek success on their feet will project their personal individuality. This takes both education and training.

Asked the difference between education and training, a professor replied: 'If your daughter came home saying that she had received sex education, you would doubtless be pleased; but if she said she had enjoyed her sex training . . .'

Presenters need *education* in the basic skills of speechmaking and presentation. These are universal, ranging from voice production to microphone technique, from the skills of speech construction or presentation to the art of destroying the arguments of others. But *training* in the use of those skills leads to the creation and improvement of their own style.

True education and the best training teach students – however mighty – to make the best of their own talents. Training and practice, combined with a critical view of the efforts, successes and errors of others, help you to create and acquire a style of your own.

No presenter of ideas or maker of speeches has ever excelled the wondrous Shakespeare: 'This above all,' he admonished, 'to thine own self be true . . .' If truth is the life of style, insincerity is its death.

3 Appearances count

If self-presentation is an essential for self-preservation, then you must make your appearances count. If your presentation is disembodied, you must take special care with your voice. You have no other way of showing your enthusiasm and your sincerity, your confidence and your command of the subject.

In person or on television, you are visible. And while, for instance, dandruff may go unobserved at a meeting, on TV it stands out from a blue suit like chalk on a blackboard. So you *must* attend to such details.

Start, though, with the overall effect. How do you want to appear? Authoritative, distinguished, sound and sensible? Then wear a dark suit, with modest tie. Relaxed and informal? Then wear a light-coloured suit and maybe an open-necked shirt.

When I was first admitted as a proud member of the Magic Circle, a Midlands TV magazine programme decided to put out five minutes of '*Janner's Magic*'. I arrived at the studio to find a cape and top hat awaiting me. The backdrop read: 'The Amazing Greville!' I was urged to don the regalia of Merlin and prance before the cameras. I declined. My magic, I explained, is close-up and personal. It is an ice-breaker, delightful at dull dinners. Never, NEVER (I repeated), have I dressed up for such occasions and ('I am sure you will pardon me') I do not intend to do so this time. We compromised by keeping the unique backdrop, but leaving off the fancy dress.

That celebrated caricaturist, Ranan Lurie, once said to me: 'Your late father got his appearance right. A combination of pointed head, central bulk and, above all, of red carnation which made him instantly recognisable. You, alas, are simply a pleasant and happy looking individual without even a treble chin.' I convinced him that if he looked more closely he would see that I have at least six arms, most of them working at the same time. And I now do wear a carnation.

Whatever *your* magic, use it. Examine first your total image and then create it by your appearance. Start at the top and work down. Do you cultivate a polished head (Neil Kinnock) or bushed hair (David Ben Gurion)? Do you groom your crowning glory (Margaret Thatcher) or allow it to dominate you (Michael Foot)? Do you permit your hair to turn grey or white (most men) or enjoy retaining, or even enhancing, its youthful blaze (most women)?

If you have to 'sit' for your portrait, caricature, straight drawing or painting, choose the appearance that you want for your image (unless the artist is both distinguished and determined and insists that your way will be his). Some caricaturists work from photographs, which you supply. How they tease your initial shape into their perception is a mark of their skill.

Overall appearances apart, watch out for detail. Scarlet socks enjoy radio invisibility, but will make a distinct impression on television viewers – especially if they appear from under a sober black suit. At home or on holiday, appearances matter little. But when you appear in public, you woo the public – so present yourself with pre-studied care, or take the consequences.

4 Body talk

You may usefully study Dale Carnegie's classic *How to Make Friends and Influence People*, but Desmond Morris's *The Naked Ape* and *Manwatching* should give your presentations an extra dimension of excellence. In particular, you will learn how others give themselves away through bodily indications, and how you can avoid doing the same.

For instance, eye contact is crucial to successful speechmaking, whether seated or on your feet. Lowering or swivelling your eyes, or failure to 'look people straight' in theirs are classic symptoms of nervousness. The more your stomach wobbles, the more you should hunt for a friendly face in your audience and talk to it, eyeball to eyeball. (See Chapter 52 for movement on TV.)

Keep your gestures to a minimum. They should emphasise your words, not detract from their meaning. Keep your body still when talking. Be upright to dominate your audience.

You may wish to move around, for effect or to involve your audience. Or, like myself, you may have back trouble and be able to run, jump or climb but not to stand still. Then get a high (or bar or draughtsman's) stool, or perch on the edge of a table.

There was once a judge with arthritis of the spine who could not sit still. Counsel would pause from addressing His Lordship to look down or at a book – and would then look up to find that the judge had disappeared! Careful examination revealed the poor sufferer, leaning against a wall in the corner, rubbing his back. At least he kept still while delivering judgment.

On your feet, what do you do with your hands? Use them to hold your notes; stand behind a chair and place them on its back; hold them on the lectern; even copy Prince Philip and place them firmly behind your back – but do not use them to punctuate your words or your sentences. An occasional emphasis through an upheld finger, or a counting exercise with several, but pounding the table, banging your fists, never.

The most moving example of sparing gesture at its endearing best comes from the House of Commons. It shows how you can help others through sign language. Jack Ashley, the Lancashire lad who became President of the Cambridge Union, befriended me as a

10

youngster. His Parliamentary career was almost blighted when a failed operation left him stone deaf. How did he manage?

First, he was determined to become the finest lip reader in the world. His eyes watch our lips. Occasionally he says, 'Would you repeat that, Greville?' Generally, though, he can converse with brilliant success.

Unfortunately, Jack's own voice is as silent to him as other people's. So when he speaks in the Chamber, how does he know if his words are too loud or too soft? Neil Marten – a political opponent but close personal friend – provided the answer. For years, he sat opposite and by agreed and simple gestures indicated when Jack's voice was too loud or to soft.

The effect of a gesture depends not upon its vigour or expanse. The more economic your movements, the better. If you make your presentation seated, keep your hands away from your face and your mouth. To command your audience, do not slouch – sit straight. Avoid minor, irritating gestures – from nail biting to finger or pencil tapping to rattling coins in your pocket. Concentrate on the body of your presentation and keep your own steady and still.

Your facial expression should match your topic. President Jimmy Carter used to speak with a fixed grin on his face. Eventually, a professional teacher of presentation showed him on a video screen how wicked it looked to preserve that smile when talking about, for instance, those who had died in Vietnam. He stopped.

After chairing a memorial meeting, I was admonished for smiling on the platform. My neighbour had told me a wistful and loving story about the deceased. When on show, your face must reflect the mood of the occasion.

5 Controlling your nerves

Under stress, all human beings (which term includes most presenters) must control their nerves. I have seen great athletes coughing and moaning before races; experienced public speakers shaking and trembling before a major appearance; world leaders in agony before a crucial press conference. So join the club.

Nervous tension is a necessity for the performer in any sphere. It releases that amazing and invaluable secretion, adrenalin, which sharpens and tones up the functions of body and mind. So if you do *not* feel nervous, your performance is unlikely to excel. Greet your anxiety with expectant understanding. It will be your ally.

Accepting, then, that pre-presentation nerves are an inevitable necessity, how can you control them?

First, recognise that once you start moving, they will disappear on their own. Runners may retch as they limber up, but *never* once they are in their starting blocks. Professional public speakers may shake before they begin, but once their first words ring out they stop worrying that their vocal chords will freeze.

Second, remember that your feelings are internal and your audience will not know of them unless you are inexperienced enough to tell them. Therefore:

- *Do not* say 'I am a bag of nerves . . .' or any equivalent.
- *Do* sit back or stand upright.
- *Do* pause before you start talking.
- *Do* make and keep eye contact with your listeners.

Third, avoid whatever form of nervous twitch is your personal affliction. *Do not*:

- Put your hand in front of your mouth – you will muffle your words while leaving your frayed nerve endings visible.
- Keep your hands in your pockets – a slovenly discourtesy made worse if you rattle coins or keys.
- Fiddle with a pen, jiggle your handbag, tap your fingers or rub your hands together.
- Twist your hair, excavate your ear, pick at your nose (however delicately),

12

open and close buttons of your jacket, or engage in any other of those less entrancing pursuits of the nerve-ridden.

Above all: come to your presentation prepared with adequate notes, simply laid out (see Chapter 20); knowing your case, and confident that you can deal with your subject. Your nerves can then return to their quietude and you can make your presentation at your ease.

That said, here are a few hints to help you either to control your nerves or at least not to show how you feel:

- Take whatever position, sitting or standing, that suits you best. Sometimes, you have no choice, but often you can ask: 'Do you mind if I sit?' Or, alternatively say: 'If you have no objection, I shall talk to you standing.'
- Do not be afraid to change your position during the course of your presentation. Sit back, with your rear end tucked into the angle of the chair, but do not be afraid to lean forward to emphasize a point. If standing, put one foot ahead of the other and stay still. But if you then want to move around, do so – deliberately.
- If you are superstitious, by all means keep your favourite mascot or charm in your pocket or handbag, but do not rely on it so much that if one day you forget it, your confidence collapses.
- If a pre-presentation drink will really relax you, or a tranquilliser stop you from coughing or retching, then take one. But test your reactions first on some other, unimportant day, in case you end up befuddled. If possible, avoid both drink and drugs. They dull reactions.

A man I know was wrongly charged with arson. An honest, decent person, he arrived at his trial stuffed to the eyeballs with tranquillisers. He was not at all nervous, but he never answered the questions he was asked, and was convicted and sentenced to three years' imprisonment. It took the combined efforts of an investigative radio team and another MP and myself to get him released. Tranquillisers cost him an agonising and unnecessary year in jail.

Confidence comes with preparation, practice, and training—not with artificial aids.

6 The art of the pause

The most difficult, the most useful and the least appreciated of oratorical arts is – silence. The well-timed pause shows confidence and thought. Conversely, presenters in any medium who make haste too swiftly will arrive last.

It is the interval between words, phrases or sentences that keeps the audience expectantly waiting for the next thought. The 'er' and the 'umm' are signs of a bad and aggravating speaker. Avoid them. Be silent. Once you have learned that knack, you will find your presentations much easier. You will give yourself time to think and to choose your words. If you cannot decide what to say, say nothing. Your audience will think that you are searching for the *mot juste*, even if you know you have a blank mind. Err not. Stand firm. Look fierce. Look around. And when you are ready with your next pearl, drop it.

At the start of a speech, talk, presentation or intervention, you *must* be silent until you have the attention of your audience. If you are interrupted – whether by the drop of a window, the shrill of an overhead jet or the intervention of a colleague or interrupter – wait for silence before you proceed. To pause is not the sign of indecision or weakness, it is the speaker's greatest potential weapon. It is also the one that most presenters use far too little. Remember, *pause shows poise*.

Skilled speakers always pause before important words. 'Mr. Chairman' . . . pause . . . 'Our firm can offer you two advantages, rare in our profession' . . . pause . . . look around . . . wait . . . 'The highest reputation' . . . pause . . . 'combined with moderate fees.'

The pause must not be *too* long. Just as brevity of a wait may show lack of confidence and cause the pause to lose half its effects, so too great a length may be 'ham'. To overdramatise is as bad as to underplay – it's *timing* that counts. Prepare an important speech and rehearse it, and time yourself on a stop-watch. Then time the same speech on the important occasion. It should take longer.

The most common occasions for pauses are:

- *The opening* – make sure that your audience has settled down and is ready to hear you – whether you are making a major oration or a minor intervention.

14

- *In mid-sentence* – to emphasize.
- *After an interruption* – once again, your audience must settle back to listen to you.
- *Before your last few words* – 'And now, Ladies and Gentlemen, I ask you once more to support your Board' . . . pause . . . 'so as to ensure' . . . pause . . . 'that our company' . . . pause . . . 'will continue to expand'. Pause. Look around at those from whom you expect applause. Nod. And then sit down.

Applause gives a helpful and invigorating lift to any speaker. If you did not want it, you would not speak. We all like to be liked. We all want our words to be accepted. The 'hear hear' or clapping is as gratifying to the speaker as the groan or jeer is a misery. So anticipate and deal with cheers. Fish for them in advance, pause to give time for them, then pause again before you restart your theme.

Against hecklers, do not use pauses. Instead, look around and glare. Then leap back at the interrupter. Then pause for long enough to allow the effect of the jeer to die away, but not long enough to encourage the interrupter to try again. The borderline between the effective and the defective pause is narrow.

The pause is even more vital, and less of a risk, when hoping for cheers. If you are nervous, follow the sound theatrical first-night tradition. Organise your own claque. Tell your allies that when you refer to Mr Jones and his great service to the company, they should clap: 'Be a good friend and clap when I finish the sentence about . . .' It only takes one or two people to get the applause moving. Or say: 'When Joe gets up to speak, please help me to give him a good reception . . .' This is a fair gambit. So is: 'We must give the impression of commitment to the new project. So when I say how confident I am that it will be a success' . . . pause . . . 'clap!' The pause is even useful in ordinary speech.

An audience likes to know when applause is expected. 'We are all pleased to welcome our guest of honour from abroad, Monsieur Jaune.' Pause and you will get a clap. Rush on and you will not.

The classic saying, 'silence is golden', has no more vital and accurate application than in the presenter's world. Silence can be as valuable as speech itself.

7 Sensitivity and tact

First-class presenters react to their audience. They watch them with care, coax them into concentration, convince them with themes, and enthuse them with messages. From the moment you enter the room, sensitivity is the key to stylish success. It will, for instance:

- Help you to steer the conversation, discussion or presentation in the direction you wish, especially if it has veered onto an unexpected or unwanted course.
- Guide you to the top people, so that you greet them, respect them, take care never to demean them, and, where possible, flatter them – if only by asking: 'Have I covered the points that you want?' Or: 'How would you deal with this in your organisation?'
- Enable you to invite audience intervention or participation and to make the best use of it. Just as any skilled politician will welcome hecklers (see Chapter 77), so presenters should be pleased with interventions which enliven their task and enlighten them on their listeners' interests and anxieties.
- Ensure that you avoid jargon, terminology and gobbledegook –especially in territory well known to you, but not to some or all of your listeners. Never presume that others have too much knowledge. After all, Ms X may be new to her department or Mr Y, who should have prepared the ground before your talk, may have omitted to do so .
- Assist in recognising those who would like to ask questions, but are shy to do so for fear of seeming ignorant. This applies to seniors, whom you must never humble before their subordinates; and to juniors, whose promotion depends on their listening to superiors.
- Keep humour as your ally and not use it to humiliate those on whose goodwill you rely.
- Help you to know when your audience is getting restless or inattentive, so that you alter course, style or speed, introduce a story or a joke, invite your listeners to ask questions, or simply say: 'Are there any points that need clarification, so far?'
- Sharpen your tact – so that, for instance, if someone asks a question which shows that he was either not listening or is stupid, you say, 'I'm sorry, I'm sure it was my fault. Let me try and explain again', or, 'It's a very complicated concept and I am sorry that I did not explain it clearly enough. Let me show you on a chart . . .'

If you do go wrong (make a mistake, cause unintentional offence) then apologise. Apologies tell the recipients that they were right and you wrong. It raises them in their own esteem and does no harm to yours.

Make sure that you write down any names which you may have to quote – the chairman, the managing director, the company, the guest – and that you spell them correctly. People are very touchy about their names.

Train yourself to think ahead, so that you not only watch your audience's reaction to what you are saying at the time, but think towards your next sentence, idea, theme, or change of rhythm or style.

If your listeners look at their watches, you should be prepared to move ahead on your notes; to discard cards on which they are written; and either to advance to your close or to involve the timewatcher. 'I am sorry, Mr. Brown,' you might say, 'that we are approaching our time limit. But are there any other points *you* would like me to cover?'

I once heard a computer salesman explaining to a major company in a depressed area why they should spend money on his equipment. 'We could help you to reduce your staff by 50 per cent if you buy one of our computers,' he announced. I could see each of his listeners saying to himself: 'Would I be one of the 50 per cent to go?' The contract was lost. Sensitivity matters. Some basic rules of sensitivity to remember are:

- Try not to continue with your presentation while anyone is talking. Stroll over to the disturbers of the peace. Pause. Smile and say: 'I'm sorry to disturb you . . .' which is usually taken in good part. To continue while others talk is to show inexperience and to invite inattention.
- If you do not know what your prospect requires, you cannot produce a successful prospectus. No proposal has ever been accepted unless the engagement pleased both sides. To know what the other side wants, listen.
- You may have to prod and provoke your audience or potential clients or customers into words of intent. Usually, though, they will be only too willing to talk about themselves and it is the good listener who is regarded as wise – and as worthy of confidence and of contracts.

If you wish to be chosen, know when to be silent.

These sensitivities apply to private as well as to public presentations – from person to person to a platform address. But when you are eyeball to eyeball, eye contact is both easier and more relaxed. The larger your audience, the greater your temptation to treat it as

17

remote, but the greater your need to relate your sensitivities to those of your individual listeners. Otherwise do not blame them if they take as little interest in you and your message as you do in them and their reactions. So sweep your eyes across your audience and be ready to react to them.

8   Personal experience

In general, the less you use 'I', the greater its impact when you do. Arrogance and immodesty are irrevocably united in the first person singular – and the more singular your person, the more carefully you should remove 'I' from your vocabulary.

Once your presentation has ceased to be – or at least, to appear to be – a personal plug, you can then feed in your personal experiences to give weight, colour and impact to your words.

Once you have decided to weigh in with your own stories, avoid such common insincerities as:

- 'If I may modestly say so . . .', or
- 'In my humble opinion . . .' or
- 'I do not wish to boast, but . . .'

Humbug. False modesty. Leave it out. Rather, praise your audience. Assuming that you ladle on the flattery with even minimal charm and credibility, your words will be both believed and appreciated (see Chapter 12).

Use 'yours' – and use the vertical pronoun with discretion.

9 Humour

Laugh, says the proverb, and the world laughs with you. But not necessarily if you are a presenter. So here is your quick guide to some of the major *don'ts* if wit and humour are to serve you as they should – as single-edged weapons.

The best humour is immediate, impromptu and to the point. So whenever possible, avoid the contrived; the set joke is for professional jokesters, but note how often they will 'die' on stage. Fresh witticisms live longer.

The best jokes are about yourself; the worse about others. Every racist story is likely to offend someone; and even the most harmless of their kind are only worth telling by their targets. So leave Jewish jokes to the Jews and Irish ones to the Irish. No one, of course, can object to your telling a joke against yourself.

To use humour, you must believe in it. If you do not believe that your sally is funny, get rid of it. And if you find that your best stories and most brilliant repartees are falling flat, go serious. You can always turn back to humour later, if the mood shifts.

The audience must be 'in the mood' to laugh, or humour fails. If you are lucky, you will find your listeners rising to the after-dinner occasion by laughing at even the weakest wit. Then sail in with your stories. If the mood is sombre, watch it.

Timing is crucial. Imitate the great comedians and listen to them pause, work up to a climax, then strike home, often building one laugh on to the next.

Humour must not only be at the right pace, but in the correct place – slotted neatly into the speech, talk, or broadcast – and the audience must be warned, by smile or tone or gesture, that you are joking.

The presentation of humour requires greater confidence than any other aspect of the presenter's craft. It comes only with practice – which includes failure alongside success. If your joke fails, be not dismayed, but:

- Continue as if the words were intended to be serious – your audience may momentarily wonder what you meant, but will be cast forward by your next sentence; or

- Simply say: 'Sorry – I thought it was funny!' That will almost certainly produce laughter, even if your original effort did not.

You need good luck with any sort of presentation. For successful humour, you should crave fortune in its fullest measure. As with style, so with humour: practice, training and a critical appreciation of the efforts of others provide the only true guides – plus top material. For some of that try my 'Compendium of Retellable Tales', which forms part of that (now happily standard) business book, *Janner's Complete Speechmaker*.

Wit and humour are the life of presentations and the soul of success. But they must be well and carefully used. How? That enchanting wit, Bob Monkhouse, suggests these four rules:

- You must find the humour funny yourself. If it does not amuse you, then you will not be able to put it across to others.
- You yourself must be comfortable with the material and confident of its use. The material must suit you, your style and your approach.
- The material must be apt and acceptable to your listeners. You must match material to audience.
- The material must not be offensive to your listeners. That which pleases some audiences will upset others; watch out for individual distastes. If in doubt, leave it out.

Some humour (often, the best) is impromptu, topical and lifted out of the audience, the occasion or the venue. Most requires preparation. As Monkhouse says (in *Just Say a Few Words*), 'Do your homework, research, learn, revise and organise all you can about your subject, then write it down and rehearse it; then think about it and talk about it – leave as little as possible to chance.' Which leads to his next five rules:

- Be proud – you are offering 'top quality merchandise'.
- Be welcome! Your audience want to laugh – the vast majority of them want you to succeed.
- Be sober! Monkhouse suggests using only enough alcohol to lift your morale as you prepare yourself – and no more.
- Be direct! And find someone who is apparently agreeable and a pleasure to talk to.
- Be steady! Take a few deep breaths and do not rush breathlessly into your words.

You are witty and amusing in private speech or chat? Then don't be afraid of using humour on your feet. On the contrary – remember that a humourless, or witless presentation will fail.

A fellow MP was due to give an after-dinner speech. Urgent parliamentary business forced him to cancel. He offered to try to find a substitute.

'We are very sad that you will not be able to join us,' his host wrote, 'but we are glad to accept your offer to find someone to take your place. Please would you ensure that he is, like yourself, a wit.'

My friend wrote back: 'I am very sorry but I can't find anyone to speak at your dinner with wit. But I have found two people who will do it for you and each is a half-wit!'

Half-wits are never welcome – no wit means no success. Prepare, practise and use humour, and you should do well.

10   Memory

The idea that jokes or stories simply embed themselves into the average excellent mind is as common as it is ridiculous. Top professional speakers and comedians alike hunt constantly for material, which they then record for future use.

When I hear a good joke or story, I jot it down *immediately*. From card, envelope or menu, the tale gets transferred to audio tape. The top copy produced then goes into a file marked 'Jokes' and the carbon into another marked 'speeches' – so that if one goes astray, the other remains. The original returns to my pocket and I use it. If it goes down well, I put it into my diary and my repertoire. If the tale proves durable, it goes into the 'Retellable Tales' section of my *Complete Speechmaker*.

When working on a speech or presentation, I leaf through my file and my 'Retellable Tales' and an appropriate story, joke, epigram or illustration will usually surface. Often, I put half a dozen possibles onto separate cards. These can either be used or discarded (appropriate word) to fit in with the audience and its mood.

Naturally, professionals build up a repertoire of stories for occasions. But even the most skilled use props, aids and memory revivers. Some experts cut out appropriate quotations and clippings from newspapers, or photocopy them from books. These are filed, indexed and cross-referenced. If genius is indeed ten per cent inspiration and 90 per cent perspiration, then the remembering of jokes and stories is equally the triumph of motivated mind over material matter.

11   Flattery

Flattery is modesty put to work. Think about it. Instead of saying, expressly or by implication, 'What a good person am I', you proclaim, 'What a grand person you are.'

Your listeners or correspondents may think you are tremendous, but they are unlikely to retain that view if they find out that it is shared by yourself. They will have a high regard for themselves. So cash in.

Suppose that the object of your presentation is to achieve some sort of agreement. Whether you are seeking sales or cancelling orders, hiring or firing, it matters not. You are asking your listener to agree with your sentiments and wishes. Whether or not you achieve agreement depends on all the facts and circumstances. It may also depend on whether you follow the advice in this book. There is one certainty – if you express a high regard for the character, integrity, and intelligence of your prospects, they will agree with you. Tell people either that they have no sense of humour or that they are terrible drivers, and the more accurate your words, the more they will hate you for them.

So whatever the nature of your presentation, the best possible starting point is praise. If your flattery is insincere, then make sure that your reservations are invisible. If the praise is undeserved, that will make it no less welcome. If your audience are susceptible to self-adulation, then they are no less worthy than 99 per cent of their fellow human beings. We are – and we might as well face the fact – a self-centred lot. We are capable of courage, no doubt, and of putting others first, but here are some more universal propositions:

- Executives are interested in their company or firm – but their livelihood comes first. If they are to be sacked, demoted or pushed to one side, the business comes second. They and their families must be fed.
- People at all levels of management are likely to be loyal – but only so long as it suits them. If you want the secrets of your competitor, then waste no money on professional industrial spies. Just find out who was last to be fired and you will acquire most of the information you require, for the asking. Commercial hell hath no fury greater than an employee sacked.
- Your prospects may one day need you more than you now need them: a hint to that effect might do no harm.

24

Flattery is also a major weapon, crucial to the answering (or deflecting) of questions, for example:

- 'Now, *that* was a most important question . . .'
- 'Thank you, madam, for putting that question. I should have covered that point in my presentation . . .' (At best, you have given yourself the chance to look up or to remember the answer. Otherwise continue with the next one.)
- 'To answer that important question will require research. I will gladly enquire into it and let you know.'
- 'That is a *very* fair question. I wonder whether anyone here can suggest the best answer to it?' You do not then reveal whether or not you yourself could provide an acceptable answer. Instead, you involve your audience, draw them out, and with luck, someone will let you off the hook. If no one does, then at least you and they will know that you are not alone in your ignorance! You can safely promise to get the information and pass it on.

There is a nice balance between decent and acceptable flattery and sycophantic smarm. It lies in one word: sincerity. That you must never lose.

12 Audience recognition

The best training sessions on presentational skills involve people who are all at the same level (see Chapter 47 on training). No one is beholden to, jealous of, or dependent for their living on, anyone else. When lecturing in-company, I try to induce my clients to bring together people at approximately the same level. If they want to include the boss, I warn them that the atmosphere may freeze, the jokes fall flat. The participants may be too apprehensive of their living to venture into asking or answering questions when a foolish moment could lose them promotion or even their jobs.

This applies especially to learning presentational skills. Results are magic, but the stress is best shared with people at the same level. I once addressed all the executives of a catering company, on health and safety. The first part of the morning took off in a gale of laughter and I could give my message to a relaxed and receptive audience. After coffee, everything froze. I only understood what had happened when I learned that the boss had, to everyone's knowledge other than mine, joined us after the break; and that earlier in the week he had sacked 20 executives.

So if you get the chance to choose your audience, do not aim at uniformity of personality or approach but at a similar level within the organisation. If you venture into the highly personalised and difficult task of teaching any of the arts of presentation, take extra care.

You may, on occasion, have to talk upwards, either to superiors on their own or to those embedded in a mixed audience. The basic rule is: never show up anyone in the presence of his or her superior. Tread on a man's dignity, said the sage, and he will hate you for life. Make him look small or stupid in the eyes of superiors, or inferiors, and you have acquired an enemy.

If you lower people who are your superiors, they are unlikely to raise you up. If you make an idiot out of a colleague, in the eyes of your shared boss, then protect your back.

If you address an assembly of your elders, then indeed your mettle will be tried. How do you show you have more knowledge than them, without making them dislike or fear you, as a present pain or a future rival? How do you show respect without creeping; humility without being humble?

If I have a boss in the room with his subordinates, I ask him for his opinion. The subordinates get praise, not ridicule. Dignity must move in both directions.

Banter and teasing are invaluable weapons in the trainer's armoury, but use them with sensitivity or they may rebound off their target and strike you down.

Tact, sensitivity, intelligence, common-sense – you will need them all, plus good luck.

*   *   *

These rules apply especially to presentations to children, young people, or students. Have you ever been guest of honour at a school prize-giving? Or taken part in a university debate? Or given a talk about your business or your hobby, to a youth club or group? Those who talk down to the young are blighted. If you treat them as equals, then with luck they will not only listen this time but ask you again. You fail to prepare your subject at your own risk. The young are swift to spot a fraud or a phoney, and have an instinct for the insincere.

Naturally, you must adapt your style and your material to your audience and to your intent. You would not talk in the same way to your sales force as to your shop stewards, nor use the same material when explaining why pay has to be held down as you would if launching a new product or scheme.

Sales people, for instance, are an extroverted race apart. Outgoing and thick-skinned by the nature of their craft, they (like all other good professionals) only respect knowledge and expertise that at least equals their own. You must talk their language if you want them to listen. A sales force needs to know what you are going to provide for the market and when and how. It needs detail on territories and prospects; on targets, plans and projections.

Shop stewards have a different job. They are elected to look after their members and you can only reasonably hope that they will co-operate with you if you can satisfy them that your proposals are indeed in their members' interests.

Your sales force are as much employees as your workforce and their physical independence and initiative is far greater. But if the workforce is unionised, it has a different type of independence. If you are talking to union representatives, you should match their knowledge and determination with your own. Give them the maximum of information (accurate and honest). Recognise their loyalty to their union and to its members. If you can harness their members' interests to your own, you are in business.

You may have to address your managers. They are your colleagues, so treat them as friends.

There is a peculiar and almost universal belief that communication between management and unions in British and American industry is poor. In reality, it generally ranges from good to excellent. Communication collapses within management itself, getting worse the lower down the line you go, or the more varied the companies within the group.

British law encourages this sad trend. Managers are required to give information to unions for the purposes of collective bargaining. But do you bother to inform your own colleagues in management, if not beforehand, then at least at the same time? Ask most middle or line managers how they get sensitive information and they will tell you: 'We ask the shop steward. He's got access to the boss.'

Ask yourself, who has the greater access to *you*, the convenor or shop steward, or the foreman or line manager? Are you not on first-name terms with union chiefs while keeping your distance from your own middle or (especially) lower management?

When you speak to your managers, remember that they may be more disgruntled than your workforce. Indeed, some of them may be paid less than some of those they supervise. This unattractive result of employees receiving overtime, bonus rates and the like, while management must work 'for such hours as may be necessary for the proper performance of their duties' – and then at fixed rates – can cause vast ill will.

When you address your colleagues, recognise their problems, personal as well as managerial. Respect their jealousies and meet them head on. Subordinate managers work *for* you? Fine – but *you* are also working *for* and *with* them. Get your approach into focus and your presentation should succeed.

*   *   *

Few executives or managers confine their conversations, speeches and orations to their superiors. Most must at least spare an occasional word – and sometimes, a great string of them (dignified by the name of 'speech', 'lecture', 'talk', 'harangue', or 'presentation') – for their juniors.

So, recognising that even a God-like chairman or managing director must speak to those below him (and that there are very few who will talk only to Him) here are the three rules for addressing your staff, employees, workforce, sales force, or others upon whose success your own job and future may well depend:

- *Never* talk down. Patronising, condescending bosses will never get the best from their team. Instead, chat them up. Build them up. Create in their minds the knowledge that they are part of a team which you are both happy and suited to lead.
- Regard these staff or employee talks as important – otherwise why should they? Follow the same procedures for them as you do for any other notable presentation, including careful preparation. There is no one, other than your immediate family, more likely to spot, or be sensitive to, your errors, than your colleagues.
- Approach the subject matter, and your effort to put it across, from the viewpoint of a colleague or a team leader, and one whose income just as much depends upon their successful effort as their living does on yours. Together, you can make *their* business survive, blossom and flourish, but pull the business apart and it will fail – to the loss of all.

13   Making your point

A government minister announced that the armed services would take youngsters under the current Youth Training Scheme and give them 12 months' voluntary service. The Opposition spokesman made three points:

1) That the trainees would receive no technical or professional training; therefore
2) They would emerge from the services no better equipped for civilian life than they were when they went in; and anyway
3) That the entire operation was 'an insult to the Armed Forces'.

'Insult to the Armed Forces!' ran the newspaper headlines. Point 3 got the mileage; and points 1 and 2 (each of which was far more important, intelligent, profound and politically useful than the third) got lost in the small print. Surprise, surprise!

When you make a presentation, it is not enough merely to produce your points. You must *balance* them. Consider which ones are crucial and which could or should be dropped. When looking for exclusions, strike out without mercy not only those which are second-rate in their own right, but also any which will blot the others through sheer weight of sensational appeal.

Business people, like politicians, too readily blame the media for leaving out their 'bull' points. Unfortunately, it is bulls that get into the ring and cows that are left to moo in the field. If you dress your points with verbal horns and ribbons, you really cannot blame the press if they latch onto the finery. Not only should you play *down* the unwanted, but dress *up* your keypoints so that they get their fair share of public glamour.

To some extent, you can choose your own headlines by the simple expedient of writing them. If you put out a press release (Chapter 62), use the heading and the contents to suit yourself and your own intent. If you can save journalists work, they will be grateful, and your prospects of getting your message across through them will be much increased. But if your ideas are unappealing or your words drab, your offering will be 'spiked' (jargon for 'binned').

Do you sell your products by marketing them in colourless

30

packaging? No. Then don't expect to sell your ideas if you are not prepared to decorate them in attractive, or even gaudy, language. You promote your services through eye-catching advertising? Then why not press your ideas through mind-catching language?

The greatest criminals in the world of presentation are the dullards.

14   Foreigners

Whatever your nationality, the world is populated with foreigners. So when presenting them, do not pretend that foreign audiences are no more than Britons (or, if appropriate, Americans or Australians etc) gone wrong.

Start by presuming that at least some of them speak, or understand some variety of, the English language. There was once a renowned Chinese Ambassador to the UK called Dr. Wellington Koo. At a dinner, he sat beside a managing director who spent most of his time talking to his other neighbours, but occasionally turned round to Dr. Koo and said: 'Nicee soopee?' or 'Nicee meatee?', or 'Nicee cakee?'

In due course, the Ambassador was invited to address the assembly, which he did in immaculate English. When the great applause which marked the end of his speech had subsided, he turned to his neighbour and enquired, simply: 'Nicee speechee?'

So, if you wish to disparage the Yanks, or the Limeys, recognise that at least some of them are bound to understand the most offensive of your remarks.

If you are invited to make your speech or presentation in English to people for whom it is not the native tongue, do them the courtesy of at least starting and finishing in their language. However difficult you find other pronunciations, you should at least manage their 'Ladies and Gentlemen – thank you very much for your welcome', even if you have to write it down, syllable by painful syllable, on a card or menu. Don't worry if you mispronounce – your effort will still be appreciated.

The same applies to the ending. 'Three cheers for the United Kingdom!' would sound ridiculous in some circumstances, but might be well received if pronounced by a foreign guest to a British audience. 'Jai Hind!' is ideal for those who wish India to live forever – and there is an equivalent in almost every other tongue.

Naturally, you must get your overseas wording from someone whom you trust. I learned this lesson when serving in the British Army in Germany, shortly after the Second World War. A local orderly asked a sergeant how he should reply to the Major, next time that officer told him that he 'knew nothing'.

'That's easy,' said the sergeant. 'When he says you know nothing, you reply: 'Herr Major, I know f. . . all!' When the orderly duly made this revelation to the Major, the explosion reverberated throughout the British Army of the Rhine.

Now suppose that you have a reasonable command of the language of your hosts or guests whilst they have minimal English. If precision is crucial, then do them the goodwill of starting in their tongue, but then shift to English, even if you have an interpreter.

Any lawyer will tell you that it is hard enough to achieve accuracy in a language which all believe that they speak equally well. To understand the problems even of accurate translation from one language to another, diplomats will refer you to UN Resolution 242. In English, it calls upon Israel to relinquish 'territories' occupied during the Six Day War; but the French says: 'all territories'; and between the two lie war-loads of misunderstanding – of the sort to be avoided by business people with the same care as any of Egypt's ten plagues.

Still, as a wise Israeli once pointed out, at least the title of Resolution 242 has one unique advantage – it is the same if read forwards, as is normal in English or French, or backwards, as is customary in Hebrew or Arabic!

If you do need an interpreter, remember that you generally get what you pay for. As with employing any other professional, it is worth spending the extra to get the best.

Speaking through an interpreter is an excellent discipline. You are then required to keep your ideas compact, your sentences short – and above all, your speeches and your presentations to no more than half their normal length. Your words do not become doubly precious because they are repeated in another tongue, but unless the interpreter is taking a cunning shortcut, the timing must inevitably double.

After listening to a particularly vociferous, lengthy and uninterrupted diatribe delivered by Stalin, Churchill is said to have whispered to his interpreter: 'What is the old boy saying?' The interpreter replied: 'He says – No!'

The converse is practised by some skilled diplomats who understand your language while you are ignorant of theirs. They insist on two-way interpreting because they have double time to consider. 'Hurry' is an Anglo-Saxon ailment.

Someone once asked an Irish professor: 'What is the Gaelic for *mānana*?' He replied: 'We have no word in the Irish language to covey quite that sense of urgency.' When dealing with foreigners, adopt their pace, or recognise failure as the price of haste.

Vive la difference! And use it to your own advantage.

15 Timing

Time is the enemy, but judge and use it well, and your speech and presentation should prosper. Most experienced business people are expert in time management except when on their feet. Aloft in their private joy, they ignore both the minutes and the agony of their audience.

'Did I speak too long?' enquired one managing director. 'Not at all,' his host responded. 'You helped to shorten the winter!'

Whether you are making a speech or a presentation, your object is to capture, to captivate and to convince your audience. This means keeping it alive, not boring it to death. How rare is that precious compliment: 'I wish he'd spoken longer, I could listen to him for hours'? How common is its converse: 'I thought he would never stop.'

As a post-graduate student at Harvard, I debated at the famous Norfolk Penal Colony. My partner was Anthony Lloyd, now a high court judge. Our opponents were Bill Flynn, a forger, and Buzzy Mulligan, in for manslaughter. American debating is a taught art, with strict rules on timing, and judged by both content and presentation. We were briefed by Flynn. 'Remember, please,' he said, 'that in this place time is served, not enjoyed! Minutes, hours and days are notched up on the wall. Your audience is sensitive. Last year, we welcomed two debaters from your Cambridge Union. The opener did not start off very well. "It is a joy," he said, "to address a captive audience!" It is no fun being one!'

So respect your audience and its mobility. In Parliament, if you overrun a sensible time, you will empty the chamber, leaving behind only those who have to stay because they are waiting to speak.

To antagonise any other audience – especially one that is either standing, or seated in comfort – all you have to do is to speak too long. Work out your timing in advance; adapt it to your audience; and keep in touch with them while you speak.

A vicar found only one parishioner at his evensong service. With grim determination, he followed the prayer book to the letter and included a splendid half-hour sermon. When all was over, the vicar shook the sole listener's hand most warmly. 'Even if there is only one cow in the field,' he said, 'he must still be fed.' 'Indeed he must,' replied the parishioner. 'But you don't have to give him the whole load of hay!'

In general, the smaller your audience, the shorter you should keep your presentation. Use the extra time to communicate, listen, invite and answer questions, and establish and keep rapport. Your object is to win friends and to influence business? Then do your audience the courtesy of including them into your time calculations.

Do you recognise the importance of time in your business? Perhaps you operate that inherently inhuman 'clocking' system, for your workforce and maybe even for your junior management? Perhaps you regard this as part of the necessary discipline of commerce. Then at least apply self-discipline to your own utterances, otherwise you will be talking to yourself, metaphorically if not literally.

Start by arriving on time. I once heard presidential candidate, Adlai Stevenson, apologising for turning up late at an election rally. 'I am deeply sorry. There is no greater thief than a man who steals the time of another. It is the only commodity that can never be recovered.'

Plan the timing of your presentation. Recognise that while time creeps slowly for the prisoner, it races for the speaker. Concentrating on your subject and your audience, you will not notice the passing minutes. Always underestimate the time you need and you will seldom be wrong. If you are preparing a half-hour presentation, then plan for 20 minutes. You can always use the balance for questions. Ask the chair – or even a colleague or confederate in the front row of your audience – to give you a signal when you have, say, five minutes left. Do not wait for the gavel to descend or the light to flash.

A well-known politician hideously overran his time at a dinner. The next speaker whispered to the chairman: 'Can't you stop him?' The chairman lifted his gavel but it slipped from his hand and hit his neighbour on the head. As the poor man slid under the table he was heard to exclaim: 'Hit me again! Hit me again! I can still hear him!'

I use a watch with an alarm. I set it for five minutes after my speech is due to end. I am happy that it has yet to sound off. If you do not have a watch or clock within easy view, you must consult the time with due cunning. A glance at your wristwatch will be noted by your audience – which is at least less disconcerting than your audinece looking at theirs.

A vicar once said to an inattentive parishioner: 'Now, Mr. Brown,

I don't mind when you look at your watch during my sermon. But when you take it up to your ear and shake it . . . !'

Queen Elizabeth has elevated the art of surreptitious watch-watching to its ultimate. She wears hers on her right wrist, facing inwards. When she holds out her arm – whether to shake hands, to lift her cup, or even in a simple gesture – time appears before her eyes.

Keep your eye on the time and your listeners will be grateful.

16   Interruptions

How should you handle interruptions? It may be the chairman of
your prospective company client, wishing to intervene with a
question when you are in full and eloquent flow. Do you say to him:
'Would you be kind enough to let me answer at the end?' Do you
thank him for his query: 'I am delighted to deal with that important
point . . .' Or do you say: 'I shall be coming to that crucial question
in a few moments, if you will permit me to do so . . . ?'

Skilled speakers welcome interruptions – in the right places. Apart
from giving the speaker the chance to show his mettle, the heckler
can rouse the audience and put them on the speaker's side. The
unexpected break can bring variety to a dull occasion and spark off
an easy burst of laughter – and sometimes, the interrupter may make
a point better than the speaker can. But you have to be alert to reap
the benefit. If you are tied to a script, written or memorised, you may
be thrown off balance. If you cannot think on your feet, you are
better off seated.

First, take the heckler. The shareholder comes to a company
meeting to criticise, and constantly interrupt you. How do you deal
with him?

Maintain your dignity. Quiet but firm appeals for a fair hearing
usually bring applause. 'I appreciate that you have a point of view to
express and you will be given your opportunity to do so. Meanwhile,
I would ask you to have the courtesy to listen.' Alternatively: 'If, sir,
you would be good enough to listen to what the Board has achieved
in the present difficult circumstances, you might learn something to
your benefit.' If the moment has come to be rude, try: 'If you would
listen to me, sir, instead of to yourself, you may be doing yourself a
favour as well as the rest of us.' Or, simply: 'Have the courtesy to be
quiet.'

Naturally, if the meeting gets too rowdy and you cannot control it,
the Chair must intervene. If you cannot deal with the interrupters,
the Chair may ask them to leave. Still, it is rare that wide-awake
speakers cannot keep audiences in reasonably good humour, or at
least get a hearing.

Some interruptions are healthy and helpful, whether or not that
was their intent. Humorists' outcries can often be turned against

them, assuming that the speaker is alert. The scream of a jet engine overhead may drown you for the moment, but give you the chance to draw some moral about the point you are making. Even a friendly remark addressed to a member of your audience arriving late may save you both from embarrassment, as well as giving you the moment you may in any event need to sort yourself out – to vary the pace of your talk and give your audience the chance to relax, to shift about in their seats and to prepare for the rest of your presentation.

Self-confidence is vital. You must appear to be in complete command. The more you feel like panicking, the more you must smile, pause and give the appearance of absolute 'unflappability'. The rowdier the meeting, the more disconcerting the interruption, the more aggravating the break in your train of thought – the more you must take care not to be thrown off your guard.

At any first-class political meeting – if you can find one – watch skilled politicians at work. Listen to how they prompt their audience to get cross with hecklers; to tell them to 'shut up'; to demand from others in the audience that they give the speaker a fair hearing. Half of a good political speaker's work is done for him or her when there are a few inefficient hecklers in the audience.

The more spontaneous the reply, witty the retort, speedy the counter-attack – the more effective the speaker and the speech. A weak riposte now is better than that brilliant barb which you afterwards wish you had thought of at the time.

So do not be put off your stroke by interruptions – use them.

PART II

Visual aids

17   Visual aids and accessories

Words are the essence of presentations. Visual aids and accessories are methods designed to aid and assist presenters. They should supplement, but never supplant, your words. An aid emphasises the vital, and explains the complex. It adds colour, variety and style. It must be selected with care and used with skill.

In the following chapters, we take a brisk look at audio and visual aids, and at films and discs and other selling and training aids and accessories, which can, usually are, and often should, be used either on their own or with a brief presenter's commentary. First, we consider those props which direct the eye to supplement the ear – accessories designed to bring and to keep the audience to its varied senses, and (if I may mix the marvel of metaphor) also keep it on its individual and communal toes.

Remember, human minds differ – some people can absorb ideas from letters and books, other from lectures and oral lessons. Some minds are photographic, others assimilate through action. Some who are highly literate are totally innumerate – and *vice versa*.

Slides and tape-slide presentations

Slides can be presented in many different ways – from the simplest single projector and portable screen, to the computer-controlled, multi-projector systems often used in fashion shows.

One useful alternative to the single projector and screen is to use a self-contained, desk-top machine. These machines project the slides internally onto a small screen at the front, which is usually about the size of a TV screen. They are only suitable for a small audience, but they do not need any black-out. They are usually portable, as no screen is required.

Another possibility is the 'dissolve pair'. The slides are split between two projectors so that the presenter can fade from one to the other and eliminate the blank screen between slides. The two projectors are mounted side by side or one on top of the other and are controlled by a 'dissolve unit'. A simple hand control advances the slides. Most dissolve units may be controlled by a pulsed tape. (This also applies to the desk-top machines described above.) They allow the operator to record a commentary, and then to pulse the tape to advance the slides at the correct points. With the system set up in this way, you can just start the tape and let it roll, in the same way as a video.

There are machines available that enable you to make the tapes yourself commonly called 'tape-slide presentations', but for best results do get professional help – especially with the sound track (see Chapter 19).

Keystone

When using an overhead projector, take care not to project a distorted picture. Make sure that the machine is square to the screen. If screen and machine cannot be on the same level, incline the screen. This should reduce the 'keystone' distortion, ie, widening of the image towards the top.

Make sure that all machinery is tested and ready for use (films laced up in the projector, videos advanced to the start point, slide trays set at zero) before you begin your presentation.

Note on 16mm films

Around 90 per cent of 16mm films have what is called an 'optical sound track'. Others have, instead, a magnetic sound track – in which case, ensure that your projector is capable of replaying, as not all film projectors have this facility.

18 Transparencies, view charts, slides, flip charts and other aids

There is an art to all excellence – not least in the use of visual aids. So why is this use so seldom taught? Consider – and refer to – the following points when using visual aids:

- Select the best aids for the particular occasion. 35 mm slides, for example, are splendid for large audiences and for showing pictures.
- Do not use visual aids to replace your verbal message. Charts, etc., should either: a) provide the skeleton for your presentation, so as to attract the eye and direct the mind (later to revive the memory); or, b) illustrate and explain, through graphs, etc., concepts and/or detail which cannot be explained simply, adequately and/or swiftly in other ways.
- Overhead projector transparencies are cheaper and easier to make than slides and can be drawn on during the presentation. But they should be treated with respect – their contents should be carefully thought out and the transparencies themselves professionally produced. (These sheets of clear plastic, usually mounted in card frames, are also known as transparencies, slides or overheads.)
- Keep the wording on all visual aids to a sensible minimum. This does not mean putting one simple sentence onto a separate transparency – but avoiding a mass of hard to assimilate material which is properly divisible into two or more projections.
- Transparencies, etc., should be concise, compact and uncluttered. Use abbreviations and symbols to summarise and to emphasise. Use artwork sparingly and for *results*, not *effects*.
- Remind your graphics department to make the slides with backgrounds clear and light – not obscure and dark. The darker the background, the poorer the view. Green, blue and black come out well on a white background, as black does on yellow. But red on green, or green on red, are even worse than white on red, orange on black, or red on yellow. Clarity of overhead vision should never be sacrificed for artificial and artistic impression. Best: use black on white, or white on black.
- Use 'funnies' sparingly. Humour is much better presented orally, if only because you can quickly move on and away from a failed joke. If you must use cartoons, caricatures or illustrative, graphic humour, then make sure that it is thoroughly professional.
- Choose your overhead projectors or machinery with care. For instance, I dislike those projectors with fans that change the atmosphere when they

come on; often do not go off along with the light, and disturb speaker and audience. Watch out especially for those that blow air out sideways, whisking papers all over the place. Better (in any event with a smaller audience) to use a mirror-type, fanless projector.

- Make sure your visual aids are properly set up before your audience arrives, ie, focused and with the first slide, transparency, etc., in position.
- The first slide or transparency should generally provide an overall summary – to which you can (especially with transparencies) return, filling in the detail by your further projections.
- To point at a slide, you must use (and have ready) a stick or other pointer. For a transparency, you have three possibilities, which can be used in combination, for variety and as required:
  1) Point with a pencil, pen or even a finger on the slide itself, casting the shadow of the pointer onto the screen. Put your pen down on the transparency. Do not hold it, or the slightest jiggle or movement will create a major flicker on the screen.
  2) Use pointer or finger on the screen itself – but beware of casting the shadow of your body onto the screen at the same or any time.
  3) Use a sheet to cover up that part of the transparency that you do not require the audience to see – and then move it. (I do not use this method because it irritates audiences, who find themselves wondering what is hidden, rather than thinking about what is revealed.)
- Changes of transparency should be slick. Hold the replacement in your right hand; remove the existing transparency with your left and put the new one in its place, all in one movement; and practise until you can put the replacement into a firm, central position without fiddling.
- Ensure that all the audience can see the machine – if some cannot, then move them or the screen.
- Be deliberate – do not jog, jolt or jiggle an item on the screen.
- Talk to your audience, not to the machine – and even if you are reading out what is on the screen, do not turn your back on your audience or put your face down to the machine. Try never to turn your back on your listeners.
- Minimise your own movement and that of the visual aids. Do not distract from the content.
- Use variety in your visual aids – different types, colours, underlining, etc. Visual aids should stimulate interest and not simply provide a technical message. Check your pens or crayons in advance. Break up the script by using different colours. Make sure the lettering is large enough to be seen. Use as few words as possible. For instance, do not say 'replaced by' – simply cross out whatever it is that has been replaced.
- If you draw on transparencies, use water-based pens, which can be rubbed out with a damp cloth – not those that require spirit for removal.
- Watch good teachers using blackboards, and use the techniques with your flip charts. Good teachers will ask their audiences questions while they write; never remove their eyes from their class for more than a few

seconds; and turn sideways when writing, never turning their backs to their audiences for longer than necessary. A mnemonic may help you to remember this: The three Ts – T-ouch the writing; T-urn to the audience; and only then T-alk.

- If you show slides, try not to keep the room in permanent gloom while you talk (unless you would prefer not to know when your audience slides off into slumber). Maybe you can place yourself to one side or under a spotlight, or at least turn the light on when the slides are off. Consider reserving slides for start and/or finish, or for one central episode, and leave the light and emphasis on yourself for the rest of the time.

- To avoid the blank spaces of darkness and silence between slides, you could try a 'dissolve pair' projection system (see page 41). However, these prepared slides have to remain in the same order and there is no way in which you can shuffle them. Inflexibility may be a high price to pay for apparent slickness.

- Beware of over-preparation – the over-professionalism too often produced by specialists, for the use of amateurs (auto-cued, word-perfect script, dramatic music and lighting) may be too slick (as well as costly) and will remove your personal impact, which is what distinguishes you from your competitors.

- To make the best of slides, overhead charts, etc., why not provide copies for your audience? This saves them writing, so that they can concentrate on your presentation. As with all other documentation, consider carefully whether you would wish to supply in advance (not generally recommended, because busy people seldom do their homework, and often forget to bring it with them on the day); at the time of presentation for use during its course; or at the end of the presentation, to take home.

The old-fashioned but worthy flip chart will never go out of fashion. At its simplest, it consists of a stack of newsprint attached to a board. With pens or crayons, you illustrate your words, flipping over or tearing off sheets. You may use and re-use prepared flippable charts. (I sometimes use a helpful variant – a white-faced, steel board with magnetic lines, spots and dots, and coloured, water-based pens that write and erase with ease.)

When pointing at a flip chart – as at a transparency – use your nearest hand or arm, so as not to have to twist your body and turn your back on the audience. The 3Ts (see above) apply as much to flip charts as to other forms of presentation.

45

19   Audio, video, film and disc

To make a presentation permanent, you may put it into type or print. You should also consider the magic of recording – on audio or videotape, on film or on disc. Each is a highly specialised art.

Audio

The beauty of an audio cassette is that listeners can play it at their convenience – at home, in the office or (even more likely) in the car. Then they can replay any part that particularly attracts, repels or baffles them.

At its simplest, you may make your cassette by talking into your tape recorder and leaving it to anyone of minor technical talent to copy. At best, though, your cassette should be professionally made in a studio, with a script prepared along the same lines as radio broadcasts (see Chapter 48).

For a sales cassette, you may manage with minimal voices and rely on the novelty and interest of the material to attract your market. But do recognise the script-writing and recording of these cassettes as skilled arts. The fact that you are capable of speech no more qualifies you to produce an audio cassette than your ability to press the button of a simple camera will turn you into an expert photographer.

If you make an audio presentation, get expert help. Find a good (preferably recommended) studio, and match the presentation to the content. The time that the job will take depends on those making the recording, both readers and technicians. Some fluffs are certain. The recording engineer will stop you from time to time and make you repeat sentences – if only because, for example, you 'pop' a 'p', so that it sounds like gunfire. If you and other presenters are fluent and relaxed readers, you should be able to make a 60-minute tape in three hours of studio time. If you are afraid or inexperienced or both, you should set aside your day – especially if you want to be in on the editing.

The studio will edit your cassette, sending you proof copies. Check them with care, but amend them with discretion. To return to the studio costs time and money. Once the proof is approved, production should be swift and painless. Repeat orders are cheap. As with printing, so with taping – the first copy costs more than the next 500.

If you are serious about hooking listeners to your material, look into the costs of cassette presentation. The fact that few UK companies make money from business audio cassettes should not deter you from using them as an appropriate vehicle for your needs.

Finally, if you cannot find the right people to use their own voices, try employing professional speakers. This may save on studio costs and give better end results.

Videos

Do not underestimate the importance of a video presentation. It can be shown at a press conference on a very large screen (five feet diagonal). Any number of copies can be made relatively cheaply. And it can be used for all sorts of other purposes, including showing on the company stand at an exhibition. It is also ideal for staff training and internal presentations – nearly all boardrooms now have video equipment.

Employ experts – your own or outside – to bring in and to operate video equipment. They will know that a video monitor is much better than a television set, and easier to operate. No tuning is needed and the quality is better. They will attend to your lighting, advise you on tape format, and either show you how to operate the equipment with maximum ease, minimum irritation and breakdown, or do the job for you themselves.

If you make your own, always talk to your audience. In this situation, it is the camera. Do not look away from the camera when the 'take' has finished. This is difficult to get rid of in the 'edit' and may ruin an otherwise excellent shot.

When presenting a video, make sure your audience can see and hear it. One TV screen for an audience of a hundred will obviously not do. For larger audiences, use a number of screens or one of the many available video projection systems. The same also applies to film projection – match screen size to audience.

You may wish to use video systems abroad. There are three main types of television used throughout the world:

● PAL – UK, most of Europe and the Far East, excluding Japan.

- SECAM – France and the Middle East.
- NTSC – The Americas and Japan.

These three systems are *incompatible*, eg a PAL/UHS tape will not play back on a NTSC/VHS videoplayer. There are, however, multi-system machines available, which can play back tapes of a number of different systems. So when replaying a tape abroad or a foreign tape in the UK, make sure tape and machine are compatible. (Beware of taking your own video system abroad with you. It may not work on the overseas mains electricity system.)

Your copy of the finished video will probably be on one of three formats:

- VHS,
- Betamax, or
- Low-band 'U'matic.

Of the three, low-band 'U'matic gives the best reproduction. Make sure that you have the right machine for the tape.

The best way to make a video or film presentation is to get someone else to do it for you. Otherwise you could be in for a period of massive boredom. If you are lucky, you may emerge among the stars. More likely, you will just sympathise with those who are.

Whether your efforts are to end up on a video tape or on a film, the process is much the same. Unless you are simply filmed or 'videoed live' – in which case you can leave the worrying, editing and promotion to others – you will end up in a studio.

I once spent a miserable week making a series of video tapes on the law. My script was rolled in front of me on a 'prompter', which faded the miseries of memorising. I at least knew enough to do exactly what I was told. 'Take One' was a disaster because an aircraft went overhead. 'Take Two' was scrapped because my chair squeaked. And after two perfect performances, I ruined 'Take Three' with a major fluff.

For day after boring day, we took and retook, taped and retaped, edited and re-edited. 'Never mind,' said the producer 'everything will be all right on the night!' Only our senses of humour saved us from suicide. The crew did not take themselves too seriously – which was just as well, because it turned out that their jobs were only as secure as the enterprise, which was *very* shaky.

A video is a helpful training aid, whether for role-play work, or for making or using a recorded presentation. If you need to talk to your own colleagues or workforce and they are widely spread, then forget the frills and the fripperies. Call in an operator to place a machine firmly before you – then talk to it. Imagine that you are doing a presentation 'down the line.' Talk to your audience as if they were in the room and you may save yourself a good deal of trouble and travel.

Video Shows

Discs

For private and commercial presentations alike, the disc (or album) has been overtaken by the cassette, audio or visual. If you use a works band or office pop group to create your image, then ship them off to a professional studio. Presentations on discs are for professionals only.

Hybrids

An alternative to a full-blown film or video is the series of stills, linked and illustrated by speech. Comparatively cheap, they may also be extremely boring, and, like all forms of visual aids other than the simplest transparencies, they should be left to the experts. If they are worth using, they are also worth the expense of professional production, whether by your own team or by outside specialists. Poor quality visual aids are scarcely an indication of a top quality presentation.

Many major companies use hybrids to great effect, to communicate with their staff as well as with customers, agents and others. By combining filmed interviews, illustrative film and stills, they save the time of the executives interviewed, as well as avoiding misinformation, beamed in at those who need to understand it. *Basic rule*: the more you are prepared to spend on the production, and the more professional the producers, the more effective the results.

20 Notes, quotes and statistics

Notes are essential reminders for all presenters. Even if you do not use them, the knowledge that notes are to hand – or in hand – gives crucial confidence.

They should be kept to a minimum – the first sentence; the last sentence; and the skeleton. They should contain the flow of ideas; the thread of the speech; reminders of themes; and brief headings for the eye, to direct the flow of speech but not to interrupt it.

Except where you must indulge in quotations, the shorter and clearer the note, the better. Divide up the note, using block capitals for headings, and underlining in different colours. Set the notes into columns, and lay them out so as to catch your eye, just as you seek to lay out your speech to catch the minds and imaginations of your listeners.

Notes are best made on cards, preferably not larger than normal postcard size. Each theme, paragraph, or arrangements of ideas can then be put onto a separate card. Use one side only; when the ground on a card has been covered, turn it over.

If you run out of time, you can simply skip two or three of the less essential cards, or just summarise them in sentences, and turn them over at speed. They provide your guide without restricting you to an itinerary. They leave you room to manoeuvre, and the ability to think on your feet.

In case you drop your notes, number each card clearly, at the top right-hand corner.

Notes should be guides and pointers, not crutches or stretchers. Holding adequate, brief, memory-jogging notes will give you confidence. But do not look down at them for words, ideas or concepts that you really should know. Indeed, never talk while looking down at your notes. Pause . . . look at your card or page . . . then look up and carry on.

Flexibility is vital. Be prepared to shuffle your ideas and re-order your notes up to the moment when you rise to your feet – and even as your themes unfold. This is only possible where notes are on cards, with one idea, theme or argument on each. It is impossible where a speech is written out.

Use quotations with discretion, and keep them short. To quote at length from memory is a form of 'showing off' which is seldom appreciated! – you are not performing a soliloquy. To read someone else's words is seldom a good alternative to putting thoughts and ideas into your own words. The reading of presentations – or even lengthy parts of them – is usually an error, compounded when the ideas and words are not your own. Only use quotations if they are particularly apt. To thrust an inappropriate quotation into your presentation, merely because you have a fond feeling for it, is invariably a mistake.

By all means attribute the quotation to its true author, if you can. If in doubt, try: 'Was it George Bernard Shaw who said . . . ?', or 'I think it was Oscar Wilde who once remarked that . . .'. Or if the attribution is to someone in your lifetime, you can seldom go wrong with: 'I once heard President Ford remark . . .' or 'Did you read the saying, attributed to Mr. Kruschev, that . . .' Who is to prove you wrong?

Make sure that your presentation really is strengthened by putting the statement into quotation marks, and as coming from the particular author. When trying to convince a local audience to adopt an overseas practice, it is somtimes better to adopt the transatlantic arguments, without stating their origin. Use the foreigner's arguments, but if you can and must put them into quotation marks, try, 'One great American is said to have remarked . . .'

The best quotations, of course, are those from the mouths of your opponents. 'Today, Mr. Jones condemns amalgamation. But who was it who said, just two years ago – and I quote: "Our future depends upon achieving amalgamation. We cannot survive as a small, independent unit"? None other than my friend, Mr. Jones!'

Quotations from yourself should be avoided. 'Did I not say, six months ago, that . . .?', or, 'May I repeat what I said at our trade conference last month?' sound pompous and egotistical, and are unnecessary unless you have previously been accused of inconsistency and *must* quote yourself to show that you have not changed your mind. If you have something to say today, say it. Let someone else point out that you are marvellously consistent and a person whose advice should be taken. The best you can do is to make the insinuation.

You or your staff may keep files of clippings, cuttings, photographs and ideas to incorporate into presentations. These will vary from specialist material to jokes, from the product of your own research to published efforts of others.

The original creation of your material may involve some time-consuming research, plus some preparation of facts and unearthing of statistics. But if those notes are carefully filed, next time will be a walk-over (though naturally they will have to be adapted for different audiences), once you have the basic groundwork. Some speakers favour a filing-cabinet, others a metal box with files inside. Still more make do with loose-leaf notebooks for stories and quotations, ideas and suggestions. The object is to reduce your homework to the minimum. You have no time to repeat any drudgery. So, however boring the keeping of files or notebooks may be, it is well worth some effort in the present to reduce your work in the future.

* * *

Mind how you use statistics. They are in the same category as lies and damned lies. If your presentation is to succeed, your figures must at least appear to be accurate.

A queue of graduates applied for a job with a firm of city accounts. Each was asked: 'What is twice one?' Each one replied: 'Two.' The applicant who eventually got the job replied: 'What number did you have in mind, sir?'

When you present statistics, always indicate their origin (assuming you are not ashamed of it), and do not presume that others are as conversant with figures or accounts as yourself. I am constantly amazed at the number of successful business people who cannot even read a balance sheet. So steer your way between the cardinal sins of talking down to your audience, on the one hand, and conferring undue knowledge on the other. If in doubt, explain. Your audience is far more likely to be innumerate than illiterate, so supplement your words with paper – graphs and the like – and, where appropriate, with visual aids (see chapters 18–20).

21 Reading

A politician unkindly remarked that there are two classic contradictions in terms – military intelligence and socialist lawyers! I would add a third: a read presentation.

The object of all presenters should be to project themselves –which means, outward to their audience, and not downward onto a script. So do chat informally, using notes or visual aids as your guide. There are occasions, though, when reading is essential:

- Where every word must be precise – because of the dangers of misquotation or the intricacies of the subject.
- Where the occasion itself is so important that (rightly or wrongly) you decide to work from a script.

If you must read, make sure you maintain maximum eye contact. Look up as much as you can and down as rarely as possible. How can you achieve this miracle? Sir Winston Churchill prepared his speeches word for word, but had them written or typed with their beginnings zig-zagged down the page and wide spaces between sentences. His eye would then catch one sentence and tweak his memory of its wording; he would then look up to and at his audience; and when he looked down again, his mind would take his eye forward onto the next zig or zag of wording.

Nowadays, top politicians and executives often use autocues. Like the teleprompt system (Chapter 55), which runs words before the eyes of newsreaders and other broadcasters, the autocue keeps a moving script before the presenter or speechmaker. Words are projected onto plastic screens, visible to the speaker, but not to the audience. If your occasion is sufficiently important, you can hire an autocue and operator. Practise, though, before you use it, and keep a script handy in case the contraption hiccups.

If you work from paper, here is a checklist of essentials:

- Make sure your scripts are cleanly typed (preferably with large script), and always with wide margins and good spacing between lines.
- End a paragraph on the page it began on. Do not allow a paragraph (or, still worse, a sentence) to flow over from one page to the next.
- Use marks to indicate pauses, and words or syllables to emphasise. These

marks may be oblique strokes, underlining in different colours or coloured highlights. (I dislike highlights because they destroy, however marginally, the clarity of the script, and you should avoid anything that distracts or complicates the eye or the mind. Both should spend maximum concentration on the audience.)

Practise reading your speech. Know your subject and your script, and take special care over words which trip your tongue (try 'February' and 'particularly', for example – or whatever your own 'word enemies' happen to be).

Finally, take care with speechwriters. Those you use should adapt to your style. Do not allow others who create your words or phrases, or who build on your ideas, to remove your personality and to substitute their own. I trained a tycoon friend in presentation. First job: wherever possible, to wean him away from reading. Second: to get rid of his brilliant but highly academic speechwriter.

My friend has a personality of brisk and pungent words and admires intellectuals. Fine. But he had to stop paying one of them to write his speeches because they emerged totally alien to the speaker. As the writer could not adapt to the reader's natural style, the writer had to be jettisoned.

So if you must read, do so with style – your own. Learn the techniques of skilled reading, and practise and use them.

22 Tape recorders, dictating machines and preparation

Sir Winston Churchill and great actors may succeed in making written English sound splendid when spoken. For the rest of us, there are only two alternatives: either presentations must be genuinely impromptu; or they must be written in spoken style. Neither method is as difficult as you might think.

Whether you are chatting privately to a prospect, or publicly to a gathering; on radio or TV; to colleagues or staff; to Press or public, the essence of success lies in two words: *chat* and *relax*. Watch successful presenters in any medium and you will see that they chat and relax with you.

Naturally, the style of relaxed presentation will differ wildly but you must still talk *to* people and not *at* them, and try to get their minds *with* you and not *against* you.

How, then, can you prefabricate words, set them out on paper, and then read them, so that they *sound* relaxed? My method is swift and practical – I 'write' almost nothing (except when I 'top and tail' my mail). Every word in every article or book – including all those in this one – goes onto tape. My most precious working possessions are three tiny dictating machines. Why three? Because I give them such a pounding that one is usually under repair; and if the second goes wrong when I have no third one available, I twitch with insecurity.

The other essential is plenty of tapes. They are cheap enough for you to keep a supply in your briefcase, your car, your home *and* your office. When you travel abroad, take plenty: you never know when you will need them. If you do run out of tapes overseas, try borrowing from business people; if that fails, your own Embassy, or someone else's, may oblige with a loan. Better still: always take far more than you think you will need. The cost and the weight are minimal.

I keep a machine available, day or night, in office or home, car or aircraft, lobby or lounge. My machine and I are so inseparable that my wife is convinced that I shall be holding one to my lips, dictating vigorously, as I am carted off to the cemetery.

What, then, is the best technique for using a machine and how do you acquire it?

First, get to know the contraption. Most makes are basically the same – they have one working slide or button which you operate by finger or thumb, plus a gadget you press in or move when you wish to record. You push one way to set the marvel into motion and another for a pause. The third movement brings you a playback and you soon learn to regulate its length to suit your immediate need.

Danger: the tape may get lost or dropped.

Remedy: put each completed tape into an envelope or (better still, if there are papers to go with it) into plastic, self-closing (or zippered) transparent files, envelopes, or bags.

You can talk through and over your machine as though you are talking to your audience. If you write for a newspaper, you cannot imagine the readers, so you chat to the editor or to the person who has commissioned your work or who will decide whether or not it should be published. If you are preparing a speech for a meeting, you can address your audience.

With enough practice, you should forget the machine altogether. Even if, like myself, you dictate all the punctuation, you soon find that the knack becomes so natural that the science turns into an art, and the machine goes almost unnoticed.

You may find, as I did, that any other method is cumbersome, time-wasting and (most important of all) produces heavy 'copy'. The words will not always flow as you want them, but at least you rely on your moods and not those of the machine.

If your presentation is to be timed, or the number of words must be counted, you will find the indicator helpful. With mine, I can dictate a 1000-word article or chapter within 50 words either way.

Once your piece is typed, read it out – aloud, if it is later to be spoken. It has already emerged once from your mouth, so is far more likely to be well-spoken a second time than any handwritten epic. Even if you have to make massive corrections or redictate all or part of your effort, the time taken will still be far less than the same words written by hand.

If you are used to operating a typewriter, so that words flow out of your mind into your fingers and out onto the keyboard, then you should try the technique of that master letter writer, Alistair Cooke. He speaks his words over the top of his typewriter at the same time as his fingers type them.

If you are preparing an oral presentation, speak your words first and then – one way or another – get the essentials onto cards or, if necessary, onto paper. The fact that most business people and other amateur presenters do the opposite explains why so many of their presentations go awry.

If your secretary types your dictated speech or other presentation onto a word processor, then he or she will be able to correct it easily. So if you omit an idea, or forget a sentence or paragraph, dictate it at the end and it can be slotted into its proper place.

Finally, if you use a dictating machine that runs off the mains, you will save batteries but lose mobility. If you hold your portable in your hand, be sure to switch if off after use. The switch on most portables has a 'lock' position. Use it. Otherwise you may find that when you move your briefcase, you shake the machine into action. Even if you do not mind the horrific price for alkaline (and hence substantially leakproof) batteries, you will despair if the machine has no power when you need it most. And when you travel, always carry spare batteries.

23 Amplification – and microphone techniques

Talk around a table and your voice should produce enough sound on its own. Address any major gathering and you will need amplification. How, then, do you best use a microphone and make it your ally?

First, adjust the microphone to your height. Whether it is a standing or a table model, you will probably find a turning ring near the centre which – with a combination of luck and some reasonable wrist power – should enable you to fix the mike at about six inches below the level of your mouth.

Position the microphone, even if this means keeping people waiting while you adjust the cord or, if at a table, while it gets lifted over the wine and whisky. Once the position and the level are right and the mike switched on, check for volume. Talk into it. Ask, if you wish: 'Can you hear me?' but do not tap or bash the mike.

You should be able to stand (or, in some cases, sit) comfortably and six inches away from the microphone and still have your voice come through loud, clear and undistorted. If there is a scream, pop, whistle or shriek, it is too loud; if a whisper, too soft. If your voice sounds as if it comes from outer space, with Martian echo or eerie ululation, then something needs adjusting.

You may be given a neck mike. The engineers will adjust it for sound and level.

This, of course, is not an engineer's summary. It is the result of years of love-hate acquaintance with microphones. So get hold of the mike, position it, and speak out. If the sound is wrong, then stop and have it adjusted before you launch into your speech. Stay calm, saying, for example, 'Mr Chairman . . .' Silence. Lift up your voice: 'Will someone kindly switch on this marvel?' Laughter. The engineer scurries around and flips the appropriate switch. 'Thank you.' Screams and whistles from the machine. More laughter. 'There's no need to overdo it.' The engineer tries again. 'Mr Chairman . . .' Silence.

With luck and perseverance, the microphone will be put into proper order. If it is not, or if reception is intermittent or unpleasant, then you must make up your mind as to whether or not your voice will carry. Is it better to risk being unheard than to submit your audience to squeals and screeches from the machine? Think on your feet – fast.

'Are you receiving me?' you say. 'Can you hear me at the back?' Loud cries of 'no, no' and more laughter. But note: they are laughing *with* you and not *at* you. *You* have command of the situation. *You* are waiting until the conditions are as *you* wish them to be before *you* start speaking. 'I shall do without the microphone,' you belt out. 'And I hope that you will all hear me.' Applause.

One way or another, you are off – even if it is to a late and unhappy start. Your audience have seen that you have complete confidence. More good speeches are ruined because the speaker is not prepared to take his time and make his presentation with the microphone than for almost any other reason.

Once you are speaking into a fixed mike, you are limited in your movement. When you shift away from the mouthpiece, the volume falls. Turn your head either way and your words may be addressed to the entire hall but will be heard only by those at your feet. Find your distance from the machine and stay there. Within limits, you can relax, but move outside those limits and you are lost.

Lift an ordinary mike off its stand; tuck your elbow into your side; make sure that there is plenty of play in the cord – and walk, with the mike always at the same distance from your mouth. Or use a neck or tie clip mike. But take care not to trip over the cord.

Beware of radio mikes. They pick up outside interference and sometimes hit dead spots.

Experience will show you how best to make use of the microphone. Never panic when the amplifier goes wrong. Be prepared to fall back on your own voice power, if you have to – so that you are not afraid of the microphone giving out.

Finally, a word about the mike in times of disorder. If *your* Chairperson has to stand, to restore order or for any other reason, then you must be seated. 'Respect for the Chair' means giving him or her the uncontested right to command the meeting.

If you are using a microphone, hand it to the Chair – and never to anyone else. Whether you are operating indoors or, especially, in the open air, hold onto that microphone like grim death. If it gets into the hands of a questioner, an opponent, or a wrecker, you and the meeting are both done for.

PART III

On your feet and on paper

24   Thinking on your feet

If your mind works well when your body is seated, then why should it go numb when you rise to your feet? When facing an audience, does your stomach rise along with your body, your heart thump and your tongue cleave to the roof of your mouth? Then you need to study the rules on how to think on your feet and force yourself to apply them. In this chapter and the two that follow, we'll summarise some of the most important, as they apply to presentation.

Once you get used to talking upright, it is actually easier than doing so sitting down. Ask lawyers whether they prefer to address courts on their feet or from their chairs and they will almost certainly choose to be upright. On your feet, you dominate; on your rear, you are on everyone else's level. So rise: forget that your knees are shaking, and look your audience straight in the eye.

To avoid that eye being either glazed, hostile, mocking, or all three, choose it with care. 'Even in the most unfriendly audience,' a colleague MP told me, 'you can always find some old dear who'll smile at you! And if you can't, then plant one!' If you look your audience in the eye, your own nervousness will at first go unseen and then disappear.

At the start of your presentation, then, take command – of yourself and your audience. Adjust your tie and your dress before you stand, and your microphone when you reach it. Take your time before you begin. Wait for silence and full attention – then away you go. As soon as you hear your own voice, firm and friendly, you will start relaxing.

Even if you are making a formal presentation in which any false word may be slung back at you, still try to avoid word-for-word preparation. Instead, use notes, (see Chapter 20 and, if you must read, see Chapter 21 for techniques). These should be brief, clearly legible and written or typed onto cards that you can comfortably hold in one hand. Start with your opening, so that your mind will be, literally, reminded of your first words, even if these are only 'Ladies and Gentlemen'. If you run into protocol, take a leaf out of the toastmaster's book and (with his help if necessary) list your listeners: 'Mr. President, My Lord Mayor, My Lords, Ladies and Gentlemen . . .'

Next, structure your speech. Work out its main points and put each one onto a separate card. Create the skeleton of your presentation and flesh it out with words, to fit both the audience and its reaction. I once asked the redoubtable Lord (Manny) Shinwell, after a fantastic oratorical performance in Trafalgar Square, whether he usually prepared his speeches, word for word. 'Never,' he replied. 'I work out half a dozen ideas and then hope for the best. Usually, the words cascade. Sometimes, of course, they don't . . . And that, my boy, is the challenge of public speaking.' I never heard Shinwell lose on his feet. But those who read their speeches seldom win.

When you have prepared and noted the body of your speech, sketch out its ending. Your first and your last words are the most important. The first create the atmosphere and the last leave your listeners with your message in their minds. Most untrained presenters lower their voice at the end of most sentences and leave their audience on some such unoriginal and crushing anti-climax as: 'Thank you very much for listening to me.' The idea of reaching your climax before your intercourse begins is a reversal of nature! Your audience should be thanking you for addressing them.

The key to confidence is to know both your subject and your audience. The former you can study in advance; the latter will depend not only on persons, but on mood. Ask professional performers and they will tell you: 'A story or a joke which brings the house down one night may die on the next.' That is the challenge of performing – and, as a presenter, you perform from your own script.

If you prepare your speech and use your notes as pointers, then you are ready to think on your feet. No heckler can throw you off your course, if it is already variable; no interrupter can destroy your concentration, if your mind is on your ideas rather than your words. The speaker always has a great advantage over those who would destroy him or her. The audience has come to listen, and the many will not appreciate disturbance from a few.

Words matter, and gestures detract from their impact. So keep still and if you do not know what to do with your hands, press your fingers on the table or on the lectern, or put your hands behind your back.

To hold your audience, vary your pace and your material. Watch your listeners and when their attention wanders, chase them – with an anecdote or an analogy, a joke or a story. Cast your beady eyes at anyone who yawns. And don't let people talk while you are talking. Look pointedly at them. If you are free to move – with or without a wandering microphone – stroll in their direction and they will soon shut up. If your presentation deserves attention, make sure that you get it.

If you cannot be heard, then adjust your voice to the acoustics. Move nearer to the microphone (see Chapter 23), or hold it closer to your mouth. Or just imagine that the man at the back of the room is deaf – he may be.

I once studied at Harvard Law School under a brilliant and eccentric international lawyer, Judge Manley Hudson. When he could not hear a student, he would yell out: 'Take your voice and throw it against the wall and make it' – here he paused for both breath and effect and then bellowed out – 'B-O-U-N-C-E off!' Hyperbole of course, but better that your words should be loudly heard than not at all.

Once you know these rules, practise them on any willing victims you can find. You are invited to your local Rotary Club lunch? Then accept. You hear of a series of lectures at your local Women's Institute or Church Council? Then offer to give one on your speciality.

Or get yourself trained by experts. Armed, for instance, with see-yourself-hear-yourself video and recording machinery, you can learn more in a couple of compressed and comparatively painless days than you could learn in a lifetime of error, causing suffering on each occasion, not only to yourself, but to your hapless listeners, who are probably undeserving of such treatment.

Too many presenters are oratorical sado-masochists – which explains why audiences retreat from lectures and meetings to the comparative safety of radio and the box. Here at least if a presenter is not switched on, they can switch him off.

If you want to be invited back, prepare and practise to think on your feet. As one fuel expert put it: 'If the speaker cannot strike oil, then we shall do our best to see that he stops boring!' Conversely, if you speak well on your feet, others will think well of your case. Presentation is an art and the fact that too few presenters are prepared to devote enough time to its study gives *you* a vast advantage if you are prepared to be the exception to this sad rule.

25 Words for occasions

Before reading this chapter, I suggest you re-read Chapter One, to remind yourself of the principle of 'Thinking on your feet'.

Your words must fit the purpose and the occasion. But you can adapt them.

Lord Denning has one great speech. It includes six marvellous stories, and not only have I heard it achieve standing ovations from a variety of listeners, but I have most happily joined in each. Naturally, this shrewd and wily old judge shuffles and deals his pack of ideas according to his audience. But if Shakespeare can be played unchanged for centuries and singers can live off their immortal hits for a lifetime, why should a speaker be expected to produce novel material on every appearance?

Most politicians survive on a basic half dozen themes. There being (in the words of the Bible) nothing new under the sun, they lighten the darkness of others by bouts of wit; by new plays on old words; and above all by reacting to the audience and to the occasion.

Take after-dinner speeches (see Chapter 38 for more on meals and banquets). They are expected to be lively, animated, vivacious, frisky, spirited, stirring, nimble. (Never forget *Roget's Thesaurus* when you are seeking adjectival precision – it is as crucial a presenter's tool as a dictionary.) But amateur after-dinner speakers' greatest mistake is to believe that they *must* be funny, however dead the audience.

An audience may expect sparkle, especially if wine has flowed freely. But if your first few jokes fall flat, the rule is – go serious. Pick yourself and your speech off the ground by finding some way to interest your audience in commercial or other realities. Prepare stories and hope for the best – but also prepare a serious line, in case the humour flops. You can always return to humour later.

The humour itself is at its best when topical and personal – but equally, the personal joke is far more likely to cause individual affront. Offence should never be unintentional.

Not long ago, I was (for the first, and as you will see, the last time) invited to address the Leicestershire Law Society Annual Dinner. I decided to try to explain to my colleagues how lawyers *could* help their fellow human beings and *why* they are so unpopular.

As an impish beginning, I tried: 'Mr President, My Lord Mayor, Chairmen of the County Council, Your Honour, Lord Lieutenant – COMRADES!' This went down reasonably well. I then quietly tried to explain to my brothers-in-law precisely why, whenever polls of popularity and esteem are taken, lawyers are invariably next to the bottom – with only politicians coming off worse. Knowing that jokes aimed at yourself are generally best, I pointed out the miseries of being a lawyer politician. No one even smiled. A man at the sprig table facing mine yelled out in good parliamentary style: 'Rubbish!' – an expression with which he thenceforth punctuated my remarks.

At the end of my ten-minute effort, I sat down – to rapturous applause from three scattered listeners. Two of them later offered their services to help me at my advice bureaux or 'surgeries', so at least part of my object was achieved, but I wish I had managed more and in a more acceptable way. I had, of course, not adjusted my words to my audience. I had misjudged their likely reaction.

So occasions are to be used for purposes. You must decide whether or not you wish to put across a message – and if so, then how it will be most effective. Then you take a chance.

You may make mistakes. The editor of my local newspaper told me after my legal dinner that he could not understand what had upset people so much, because there was little that I had said that he had not put into his editorials. I suggested that *his* audience could turn the page while *mine* could scarcely switch off or even walk out.

Business executives, and others who address overseas audiences, must be especially careful not to cause offence. Beware of translators (see Chapter 15).

So carve your rhetorical joint to suit the occasion – but follow the general rules, such as: humour (Chapter 10); handling microphones (Chapter 24); structuring your speech (Chapter 14) and the beginning and ending of speeches and sentences on a high note.

26 Grammar and punctuation – presentation on paper

You judge an applicant for a job by clothes, appearance, by manner of speech or writing, and by style. First impressions may be vital. *If* you get to know the person, then other factors come into play – character and intellect, in particular – but at first, it is outward style that matters.

Equally, letterwriters must watch for the immediate impact of their correspondence. This means careful attention to stationery and printing, to cleanliness of type and to the skill of the typist. It also requires that the words themselves have the impact you require.

An illiterate letter should be a contradiction in terms. Grammar matters. If the writer is uneducated, unless precedents are used and adapted with loving care, the reader will know.

The best, permanent answer is for writers to become readers. Do you take pride in reading as widely as possible? The first stage to correction is recognition of failings. If writers can achieve this on their own, that's good. Otherwise, why is there such a prejudice against formal education in letterwriting and literature generally?

Style, of course, cannot be detached from general layout. Letterwriters, like athletes, must get their start and their finish just right if their efforts are to produce winners. The contents must be clear, brief and lucid – and pleasantly paragraphed. But above all, the style of the words must reflect the *intention* of the letter.

A morning suit may be a winner for the races or ideal at a wedding – but would black or grey best suit the occasion? When you go out for the evening, do you wear black tie – or do you appear in long or short evening-dress? A lawyer must wear a dark suit or dress in court – no problem there – but what do you wear when you greet a visitor from abroad? Dress must suit occasion or it may cause embarrassment, upset, or loss of business.

The words of letterwriters are the dress of their thoughts. If these words are inept, slovenly, ill-suited to the occasion, their style will destroy their impact. Style should match circumstances.

Now, let's consider some particular occasions:

68

'Between you and I', a letter might begin . . . and if the reader is a purist, there the correspondence ends. If the writer is an applicant for a job, his prospects pall.

When you write letters, your accent disappears. Your speech may bear the marks of Belgravia or Bohemia, Brooklyn or Bermondsey, but your writing receives no overtones from your voice. This may be a great asset, because, like it or not, the commercial world is largely snob-ridden.

On paper, everyone starts at the same level – pens and word processors are classless instruments. The heavily accented words which you speak into your dictating machine emerge classless, sexless and without indication of ethnic or racial origin. At least, they should.

What can be done, then, to repair broken English? I offer three suggestions.

First, read well and widely. Study the financial columns in the newspapers and the form of both companies and race horses. But fill in those odd moments on the train, bus, in the car or taxi by reading something different. Have you dipped into Hersey or Hemingway? Do you really think that David Copperfield was a character in a film? What of Solzhenitsyn or Graham Greene or Saul Bellow?

Schools all too often spell 'literature' with a capital 'L'. They sate the appetite for Shakespeare by turning the words of the unfortunate Bard into examination fodder. A pity. To write well you should read avidly – and the greater your failings as a grammarian, the more you should soak your mind in the rich wine of fine literature. There we have it again – 'literature' – the art of letters, the skills of the literate. The letterwriters who wish their words to carry impact should read the letters of others.

Incidentally, you may take this suggestion literally, if you wish. Many of the greatest men have consigned their thoughts to letters. Bernard Shaw and countless others have caused or permitted their letters to be published. Read them.

Second, listen to good speech. By all means treat yourself to records of famous speeches, if you are feeling flush (or maybe there is a record library in your area?). On a more prosaic level, when you hear the language well spoken, make a mental note. To copy the excellent is a mark of wisdom.

Finally, do not turn up your nose at formal courses, aimed at adults. If you would prefer to remain anonymous, then have one custom-made and get yourself a teacher – the money will be well spent. Try correspondence courses – there are plenty about. Remember, it pays to learn, and it is never too late to acquire polish. And while your tutors may have to advertise their services, there is no need for you to advertise that you are making use of them.

The object of a letter is to propound an idea. Whether you are buying or selling, hiring or firing, praising, decrying, apologising, negotiating – it matters not. You are engaging in self-expression, on paper. Say what you must (or what you wish) with clarity, but your personality needs expression, along with your views.

To this end, formal grammar has its place. Sentences, we are told at school, must have verbs. Not necessarily. A sentence usually has a verb. Not always. Modern writing need not follow infant lines. Classical form has its place in ballet, but so does free expression, found in the dancers' work of today. Everything depends on the work to be interpreted, the music to be followed, the story the artists portray.

So it is with letters. There is a place for the traditional style of the formal work – and for the untraditional, thrusting, vivid writing of informal thought. Don't be afraid of the lively phrase. Words may make a sentence with no verb at all. So may one word, on its own. Often. Effectively.

In general, sentences should not begin with 'and' or 'but'. But they often do. And to good effect. You are the writer – within acceptable limits, you make your own rules. Yours is the meaning to be expressed, the personality to be put across, the style to be chosen.

Punctuation is important. The full stop is called in pungent American, the 'period'. It indicates a break in the thought. A comma marks a pause. A semicolon is half a colon – and is useful for indicating the end of an item in a list. The colon comes between the semicolon and the full stop; we have a pause in the flow of·thought, but not for long. It is also used a great deal nowadays before quotation marks, thus: 'We undertake that the goods will be delivered by the end of next week'.

The dash is a useful weapon – the pause is pregnant . . . the break in the sentence (or in the list) longer than the mere series of dots . . . The dots themselves show that the thought has not ended, even though the sentence or the paragraph may have done.

Careful punctuation breaks up a paragraph or a sentence. The breezier the style you choose to adopt, the more use you will make of the dot and the dash, the colon and the semicolon. Suiting the style to the subject and to the writer means far more than the careful choice of words. They must be strung into the appropriate phrases or sentences and linked or divided by appropriate punctuation. (You should also punctuate your oral presentations by varying the length of your pauses.)

Modern usage often justifies the ignoring of ancient rules. Take the split infinitive, for example – to carefully fix, to gently remind, to kindly honour. I hate them, but that's just my personal preference.

Before you split infinitives in your letters or speech, however, you should bear in mind that the recipient of your letter – who may, perhaps, be an important customer (actual or potential) or someone else whom you wish to please – may be as prejudiced as I am.

You may please yourself about modern grammar. But if you fail to please your correspondent, you would probably have been better off not to have corresponded at all. You would not deliberately offend, say, potential customers in speech. Then do not do so in writing. Even with grammar, tact plays its part.

PART IV

In the chair

27   From the chair – introduction

The next few chapters are for the chairperson – the man or woman who takes the chair at a presentation of any sort. In the UK, 'the Chair' includes the person in it.

The Chair will take charge of the team presentation. In the formal arrangement, he or she will be faced by the Chair of an interviewing panel. Each will try to conduct the proceedings in the way best suited to his or her intentions. In general, though, the rules for chairing are constant, whatever the circumstances of the meeting or gathering.

28   In the chair

If you are taking the chair, do not underestimate your problems. There is no art less taught but more perilous than the art of chairing.

When learning to sail, you learn, before going out to sea, that a boat may capsize at any moment with the shift of wind or weight and without warning, however, calm the sea. But how many business people sail meetings out to sea, clutching their oratorical rudders and hoping for the best, without even an hour's training in the craft of crafty chairing?

The essence of steering a presentation or a meeting is precisely the same as that of steering a ship. The twin keys to success are: *concentration* and *control*.

A friend taught me to sail in a Mediterranean bay, together in a fibreglass dinghy designed for one. 'The joy of sailing,' said my host, 'is that you forget all your other problems. Take your mind off the boat for an instant and you are in the drink.' Ten seconds later we both were.

Even with total concentration, your presentation may capsize. But the more you keep your mind on your purpose and your eyes on your audience, the greater your prospects of success. You must know what you are trying to achieve. The best meetings are those in which all feel that they have had the chance to express their view; which proceed with brisk good humour; and which reach the appropriate decisions. The rarity of such marvellous gatherings is the best proof of the generally low calibre and non-existent training of chairpersons.

Part of the Chair's job is helping other speakers to relax. Conceal your own nervousness and be careful not to convey it to others. Help colleagues making the presentation, or guest speakers or others at the meeting, to shed their fears. When theirs disappear, so will yours.

If you chair a presentation or a meeting, answer the following questions:

- What is your purpose? Who will help you? Most important decisions are taken *before* most successful meetings. But if the Chair is sufficiently skilled (which is rare) the planning will be cunningly concealed.
- Have you arranged for the best *venue* for your purpose? What about the seating? Do make sure that you have an intelligent ally (the company

secretary, perhaps? Or your vice-chair?) by your side. Have you arranged for any necessary amplification? Is there good ventilation or will the audience be asphyxiated?

- What should be on the *agenda*? The meeting must cover all the essential points within the time available, which requires a written plan of action.
- In what *order* should items be taken? Do you, for instance, put the contentious problem at the start, allowing everyone to have his or her say, hope that the storm will blow itself out, and then wind up with the desired result? Or do you leave the misery until the end, hoping that by then the participants will be bored out of their minds and prepared to accept anything in return for their release from the meeting? The beckoning bar or spouse is a marvellous inducement to common sense – which, in this context, means acquiescence in the wishes of the Chair.
- Have you primed your *allies*? These will include (as appropriate): the speaker; the proposer of a motion or of a vote of thanks; the opposers of resolutions of others which you dislike; and those in your prospect's team who are on your side.
- Do you fully understand, and can you administer, the *rules* of the organisation, assembly or meeting? If the get-together is sufficiently small or unimportant, you may be able to make up the rules of order as you go along. But if you are dealing with, for instance, a company or the Chair of an established body, you will find some sort of 'rules of order' embedded by law, by consent or by custom in its constitution.

The Chair should normally sit in the centre, with the most important guest or speaker on the right and the second most important on the left. But do you want the company secretary, or other adviser, slotted in between them?

So the meeting begins and you are in charge. Or are you?

Parliament is not merely the world's most ancient arena, but potentially its most unruly. In the view of most veteran Parliamentarians, former Speaker George Thomas was one of the greatest masters and manipulators of the House. How did he do it? Essentially, by consent. 'The Honourable Gentleman knows perfectly well that he is out of order', George would chide us. Or: 'Now, now . . . The Right Honourable Gentleman is being very wicked!' The place would explode with laughter.

First Rule of Thomas: use humour to defuse. Wit rules, okay? But it should not be used to hurt, to demean, or to distress. 'I do apologise to the Honourable Gentleman,' said George.

Rule Two: if you get it wrong, then say so and you will be forgiven. If the meeting overrules your decision, smile sweetly and carry on. Do not take defeat personally or it will be treated as such, which was (hopefully and probably) not its intention. Remember the old advice: 'Don't turn around, but look behind you!' If your eyesight – or your foresight or your hindsight – lets you down, then you must mitigate the loss.

The mood of a meeting changes with the speed of wind. An Irish wit once remarked: 'Whenever you think that we have solved the Irish question, we change the question!' So if you believe that you have won your battle with your opponents, beware – they may now change the *casus belli*.

The Chair has one great asset – the wish of everyone other than the person speaking that he or she should conclude as swiftly as possible.

Former Prime Minister of Israel, Levi Eshkol, chaired a meeting. A speaker who was likely to be boring asked him: 'How long should I speak? There's so much to say, I don't know where to begin.' Eshkol replied: 'I suggest that you start at the end!'

The skilled Chair starts the meeting by setting its tone, then guides its proceedings, and brings it to an end with firmness and fairness, grace and goodwill.

A good Chair knows how to restore good humour. On one occasion, a Tory MP demanded the right to ask the Prime Minister about the actions of certain Labour colleagues. Speaker George Thomas said: 'The Prime Minister cannot answer for Members of another Party.' 'But Mr Speaker,' the questioner continued, angrily, 'it's in today's newspapers.' Quietly, George replied: 'So is my horoscope!'

A good Chair combines tact and wit. When MPs interrupted a colleague who had been droning on indefinitely, George would rise to his feet, smiling: 'It is not fair to interrupt the Honourable Gentleman,' he would say. 'He has, after all . . .' (pause for effect) 'only been speaking, *so far*, for 53 minutes!' If anything would put an end to the misery, that did.

29   Fairness and skill

The Chair must be fair. No Chair can succeed if the meeting regards rulings – including choice of speakers – as unjust. Fairness means sensitivity to the wishes of those who have been good enough to put you in charge. Dictators have no greater right than ditherers to chair meetings.

A debate must be balanced. If anything, the Chair should give preference to minority opinions and to those who express them. Far from dissenters feeling that they are unwelcome, their views should be given a careful hearing.

Of course, no one expects the Chair to be a mental eunuch. The art lies in getting your way (at least apparently) through the voices and interventions of others.

The time may come, though, when the Chair finds it necessary to give the meeting the benefit of his or her well considered bias. Unless (again, like the Speaker of the House of Commons) condemned to total neutrality on matters of politics (corporate as well as national), the Chair is expected to express a view – but not to impose it. Indeed, if that view is unpopular or the chair is under personal criticism, it is generally both wise and tactically sound to give opponents plenty of rope with which (hopefully) to hang themselves and to destroy their own case.

If, though, you look as if you are going to lose, then here is a tactical checklist:

- Should you adjourn the discussion, or postpone the debate, and hope that you will achieve a different result when heads have cooled, or that you can use the intervening time for some behind-the-scenes lobbying?
- Should you refer the problem to a committee (or a sub-committee or commission – or 'to our company secretary', asking for a report)? A Parliamentary Committee has been described as a 'cul-de-sac into which ideas are lured, there to be quietly strangled'! Company committees may have the same useful attributes of delay or death. This ploy is especially helpful when the hour is late, those in attendance irritable and anxious to be home, and ready to accept almost any reasonable solution to gain their freedom without losing their battle.
- Should you put the question to a vote? Congress, Parliament, unions and many organisations decide by majority vote. The boards of most companies and corporations operate through consensus. (More on this in

Chapter 30). Remember: once a vote is taken, you and your company or organisation will be bound by it.

● Should you lay your prestige and your position on the line by threatening to resign if the vote goes against you? This approach is an absolutely last resort, to be used only on matters of the highest principle and when you really do not mind giving up both your chair and your power.

● The art of diplomacy is to give your opponents a ladder, to climb down gracefully. Can you find one, and if so, will it be accepted?

I once asked Lord Shinwell whether it was true that early in 1948 he threatened to resign as Minister of Defence if the Cabinet did not agree to the evacuation of British troops from what was then British-mandated Palestine. He replied: 'It is untrue. I never threatened to resign. Anyone who does that loses – and I don't like losing.'

Still, if the alternative is to be left in charge of a policy which you regard as totally unsupportable or, worse, as fraudulent or otherwise illegal – or if failure to resign gracefully may, or will, lead to your forceful eviction from the chair – then it may be as well to beat the hangman to the noose, or (to use the more apt American equivalent) the executioner to that other and more lethal chair.

30 Voting and consensus

Always be prepared to call on the silent. Ask yourself:

- Is there a veteran whose advice is worth having, but who is too shy to offer it, perhaps an ex-Chair or former leader who does not want to feel that he or she is dominating successors or imposing on the young?
- Is there a 'maiden speaker' – someone who has not yet spoken and fears the sound of his or her own voice in the presence of imposing seniors?
- Is there some official who – by intelligent inclination or by hallowed customs – only speaks when called upon? Is now the time that you require his or her tactful guidance?
- Is there someone who has remained silent out of anger – and whose wrath will increase if not 'recognised' by the Chair?
- If you are the controlling shareholder and boss – or if someone else in a position of power over the future of others is present at the meeting – should you draw out a participant who stays silent for fear of retribution? Or would it be kinder to leave the person in peace and to consult privately?

Some final tips:

- Avoid humbling – especially the weak. Tread on a person's dignity and you will not be lightly forgiven.
- Apologise if you make a mistake.
- Ride out criticism. Only the deceased are seldom criticised.
- Invite and welcome the constructive critic – use cunning, humour and the common touch to destroy the destructive.
- Hope for good luck. There is, for instance, no greater blessing than to find the meeting-breakers absent. You may not wish them ill, but if they are, then you are fortunate. And without good fortune, no Chair can succeed.

31   Chairing presentations

If you are chairing a presentation, you may do so either as the co-ordinator of those who make it, or of the audience that hears it. Either way, adapt and use the rules in the previous chapters.

If you are the head of a selling team, then remember, especially, the following points:

- The success or failure of the presentation will depend to a major extent on the impression that you personally make on your audience.
- You must accept the responsibility for ensuring that your preparation and that of your colleagues and of your case is full and adequate. Delegation is your privilege, responsibility your burden.
- If you do not control your team in its presentation, your audience are unlikely to have faith in your control of your organisation in providing the services or producing the goods that you are inviting them to buy.
- While you chair the presentation, someone else will be in charge of its audience. Try to discuss with him or her, and in advance, the format of the event. The more that its actual running is left to you, the better – provided, of course, that you have worked out how best to produce the results that you require.
- Consider whether you prefer to take questions during the course of individual talks, etc; or after each; or at the end.
- Whatever you decide in advance, be prepared to alter course if the unexpected occurs, which it always will – especially if you are not prepared for it.
- If any of your team are untrained for presentation work, then get them trained.
- Remember, others will be pleased to share in your glory if you succeed, but as Chair you will be welcome to the entire blame if the presentation goes wrong.
- In the famous words of Harry Truman, 'If you don't like the heat, get out of the kitchen.' As Chair, you are both kitchen planner and chief cook. You may leave the bottle washing to others, but you are personally responsible for breakages. If you do not like responsibility, get out of the chair. And do not ruin the work of your colleagues through failure in your own command – of yourself, of them, or of the presentation itself.

The host

In the Chair of the *host* team or audience, you are essentially in charge of the group interview. You must:

- Decide what you, your team, company and organisation want to achieve through the occasion – and how best to get it.
- Make sure that you are in charge of the operation and that your guests follow your preferred routine.
- At best, agree with the Chair/co-ordinator of the presenters – or, if it is an individual presentation, with the individual concerned – so that your courtesy and charm will enable the presenters' wares to be spread out before you, to their best advantage, and for your complete and critical appraisal.

PART V

Presenting to sell

32   Selling

Presentations are for sales. I am amazed how companies, corporations, firms and individuals invest vast sums in tendering, quoting, estimating, presenting – without sparing even half an hour to rehearse their presentation, or half a day to train for it.

The general rules on presentations – including those set out in the checklists in Part VIII – all apply. Here are a few extra top tips for people who, directly or indirectly, immediately or in the long run, depend on successful presentations for their living.

- To win contracts, your prospects must have faith in you. They will be investing *their* money in *your* expertise, *your* skills, *your* products. So *your* presence and *your* presentation must inspire confidence.
- Confidence requires *faith in a team* and not only in an individual. The managing director or partner may be crucial, but (as a top construction man told me), 'When we put in a tender, they want to see the guy who will make the project tick.' So choose your team with care.
- If a team project is to succeed, it must be *co-ordinated*. So how can they have that belief if the presentation has no real chairman; no central figure who allocates responsibility for taking points, dealing with questions, undertaking research, etc?
- Confidence means *people* – and their accessories. Each must match the prospect and the occasion. For instance, should your brochure be glossy or simple, in colour or in black and white, expensive or workmanlike . . . ?
- Sellers and their goods or services should appear to be in *short supply*, even in times of glut. People value the unavailable and reject the plentiful – even if the latter is less costly and possibly better.
- *Be positive*. To make an appointment, or a presentation, or for any other important reason, do not say: 'We will call on you any time. When would suit you best?' But rather: 'We will do everything possible to fit in with your wishes, but our diary is very full. Could you manage the morning of the 14th/the afternoon of the 20th/early evening on the 25th?'
- Find out *who* will really influence the result of a presentation. It may well be someone who is not normally present – perhaps the marketing manager, the company secretary or some other backroom person. Flatter *him or her* by asking whether he or she could not manage to attend.
- Discover as much as you can about the people who will be in your *audience* and who will make the crucial decisions. Who are they and what is their background? You never know what piece of currently useful

information may be turned to advantage. Britain's Royal Family is renowned for its memories. 'I met Prince Philip today and you'll never believe it – he remembered when we'd met, three years ago –', I've heard someone say. The *briefing* of the Royal Family is brilliant.

- What will spark off the *interest* of your audience? What particular aspects will turn them on – or off? How can you maximise your chances of winning, in the particular circumstances of your presentation? If it is worth lavishing resources on preparing your proposal or your presentation, spend that little extra to assess your audience.
- In *competitive* presentations, *try not to go first*. Warming the house is an unhappy exercise and reduces your prospects of success. Unless there is a large queue, so that the audience is bored by the end of it, you are generally best going last.
- Remember that you are being watched, especially when you are not speaking. Concentrate on what your colleagues are saying; watch your eyes, your posture, your demeanour *at all times* – and be alert for the directing of a question towards you.

If it is worth expending resources on preparing a proposal or a presentation, then it is also worth sparing time for a *post mortem*:

- Were you successful – and if so, why? Your client or customer may tell you the reasons for your selection. Otherwise, try to guess.
- If you failed, what went wrong?
- Did you make a tape recording of the session, so that you can play it back? Do not keep a transcript for the record – but consider recording events so as to learn from them.

Sir Percy Craddock, when British Ambassador to China, told me why the Japanese are generally so much more successful than other nations, including Britain, in their sales presentations to that great potential market. He said: 'When the Japanese arrive, their delegation consists of people who are expert in the various aspects of the same undertaking. They complement and compliment each other. They come fully briefed and remain until the job is done and the contract landed, however long that may take.

'Too often, our people arrive in a delegation from one or more Chambers of Commerce. They compete against each other for contracts. Their journey is for a pre-arranged and limited time, much of which they spend battling with each other. No wonder they lose!' (See also Chapter 75 – Cardinal 'Don'ts'.)

33 Proposals and pitches

A 'proposal meeting' – or 'beauty contest' or 'beauty parade' – is a pleasing term for a sales presentation. You and your prospects meet; you put forward your proposal; and your deal – and, on occasion, your future – depends on the outcome. So how can you maximise your chances of success? Here are some suggestions:

- Put yourself on the side of your prospects. When doing your preparation for the occasion, ask yourself *first*: 'What will please and influence *them*?' as opposed to: 'What do we wish to put across?' The theme of the presentation should be: 'To assist *you* . . .'
- Ask yourself, do you present your proposal in writing beforehand and then explain it at the meeting? Or do you bring a written proposal with you and hand it out at the beginning so that your audience can refer to it? Or do you present your proposals orally – perhaps with the help of visual aids – and then provide a document to leave the message fresh in their minds? There is no absolute rule: all depends on the occasion, the audience and the nature and complication of the issues, statistics, etc.
- It follows that you must consider with care the form of your proposal; its wording – and whether it is intended to be 'firm' (and hence legally binding) or merely a step in the negotiation. Keep it as brief, terse and lucid as possible.
- Consider whether you should provide references written to them or offered for them to contact? Will those for whom you have previously provided your goods or services object to the use of their names and their goodwill? If in doubt, ask them.
- Take your audience through the proposal – if it is before them, by overall survey and summary, and then paragraph by crucial paragraph. If time is short or your audience restless, invite them to read all or part of it – then add your comments and take their questions.
- If you are a small group, meeting around a table, you may not need visual aids – but give special thought to a detailed paper, diagrams, graphs, charts, etc.
- Always review: background, objectives and approach; fees, rough, estimated or exact; and beam in on the particular people and audience. When you are before them: listen, watch and react.
- Ask: do you need professional help, in the techniques of winning pitches or 'beauty contests' and/or in rehearsing for important ones? If so, specialists are at *your* service.

With these particulars in mind, now review the general rules on presentation in Part I.

34   Sales conferences

However brilliant your research and development, your productivity and your production, your industrial relations and your financial operations, no sales means no business. So the sales conference is a vital gathering.

By definition, you are presenting and selling to sales people. If they themselves are not experts at presentations, they should be. As artists, they will also be critics, by instinct and by intent. So treat any presentation to your sales staff with extra respect. This means you must:

- Identify your object, and prepare, put across and limit your message.
- Prepare your presentation – and decide (as usual) where, when, how and by whom it is best made.
- If, for example, the conference is in connection with a product launch, see Chapter 36; and if for some other specific purpose, track it down through our contents and/or index – and follow and adapt the rules; consider and reconsider the checklists.
- Lead by example – and enthuse your colleagues through your own energetic sincerity.

Any presentation made to colleagues, staff or workforce is an effort of leadership. If you cannot – perhaps through training (Chapter 47) and practice – acquire the art in your own right, have the modesty and good sense to delegate to someone else in your organisation who can. Or if you cannot refuse an instruction to address the conference, or to make or chair the presentation, and you doubt your own ability, find a way to get the training you need. It is far better to admit your limitations in advance than to have them drawn forcibly to your attention at the presentation itself and thereafter. Horses for courses and presenters for presentations – and sales conferences – should be led by those whom sales people will respect and follow.

Finally, ask yourself and your colleagues: are you getting full co-operation from all sides of the business, in the process of selling? When one department lands a contract, do they try to involve others and to extend the profit? When selling, do they co-operate in joint presentations? Or are they competing against their own company or organisation?

35 Tenders, estimates and presentational costs

As competition increases, so does the effort and expense lavished on a tender, an estimate or a quotation. Dollars, pounds and pesos are lavished on the work of the estimating department, draughtsmen, printers and the rest. Then their product is handed over to the presenters, who may promptly squander the entire investment with an ill-conceived, under-prepared, poorly thrown together presentation. So:

- Do you cost out presentations in terms of preparation, documentation, visual aids, presenters' time?
- Have you compared the resources spared for a proposal, quotation, estimate or tender, as against those begrudged for the presentation itself – training, preparation, rehearsal, documentation, visual aids, presenters' time?

If you have carried out this exercise, did you note with satisfaction or with concern the modesty of the expenditure on the presentation, as opposed to the expected and approved cost of the estimating?

If you increased your expenditure on the presentation by 50 per cent, what percentage would that add to the overall cost of the effort to win the contract? And would not your chances of success be increased by a far higher percentage? For instance:

- How many of your presenters are properly trained for that crucial function? Is your Chair, managing director or chief executive a superb technician, administration, business person – but a poor presenter and either unwilling to admit inadequacy or unprepared to learn? Do you or your colleagues underestimate the need for skill in selling so that others prepare? Do your subordinates say about you (as so many complain to us about their bosses), 'We can get him to attend the proposal meeting (or as the case may be), but not to learn how not to mess up his part in the operation'? Are they unwilling to tell you the truth about your poor performance because you hold their prospects in your hands?
- Have you ever had the necessary modesty to enquire whether you are not one of those top people who ruin your colleagues' presentations because you may be a genius at your job, but are unprepared, untutored and unsophisticated in the art and craft of the presenter?

Do you lead your team to unnecessary failure? How much time and effort do you and your team put into any of the following crucial tasks:

- Advance planning and preparation for presentations?
- Discussion and consideration of, for instance, which colleagues should make the presentation; what part each should play in it; who should chair and co-ordinate; what form the presentation should take – including when you, and/or some-one else, should deal with questions (and how).
- Who needs training for the job? Who will provide it, and where, when and how?
- Can you cope with your presentational training through your internal resources or do you need to bring in outsiders – either to provide the necessary skill and experience in the training itself or because their criticism will be more acceptable and accepted than any from a colleague, whether senior or junior to the presenter-trainee?
- Are you satisfied with your arrangements – internal or external – for the preparation of transparencies, slides and other visual aids?
- Do you set aside any (or any adequate) time for rehearsal? If so, then do you use your trainer (internal or external) to criticise your embryonic effort – or do you leave discussion, review and debriefing until after the presentation has failed?
- Indeed, do you take any (and if so how much) time and trouble to review the presentations after they have succeeded or failed, so as to consider the reasons for the results (good or bad) – and hence how you can avoid the errors that have given your competitors the edge and the contract?

If the answer to any of these questions is unsatisfactory, then join the club of commercial wasters – people who spend freely on preparation of estimates, tenders and quotations, but little or nothing on the crucial presentations that will decide whether or not the rest of their effort is thrown away.

There are certain nations well known in the world of international politics and bluster which spend imperial fortunes on armaments, including the most sophisticated of aircraft and other weapons. But when it comes to war, they do not possess the trained and motivated manpower, skilled and able to put the hardware to its devastating purpose. You could lose business as they lose wars.

36   Launches

Launching a new product or service? Then you will devote time, thought and great resources to its development, preparation, production and marketing. Do not begrudge that little extra, to produce full impact through formal presentation.

The launch is an event. Consider how to make the most of your opportunity. For instance:

- Should you call a press conference? (If so, Chapter 61 will guide you.)
- Can you get time on radio or TV? (If so, check the advice in Part VI.)
- Is your launch aimed at one or more identifiable customers or clients? If so, you will require a personal or group presentation. (Read and check Parts V and VI.)
- New products of any importance need detailed presentation on paper. Prepare your brochure and documents with care. (See also Chapter 62 on Press Releases.)
- In any formal presentation of a new product, you will require visual aids. (Their variety and use is explained in Part II.)

Where possible and appropriate, you will, of course, wish to produce and demonstrate the product or service. Consider how you can do this to best advantage. Should you invite the media and customers to your works or other premises? Should you bring the media to your customers? Or can you only demonstrate your case best by document, diagram or photograph, supplemented by explanation? Are you sure that you have chosen the right moment for the launch?

Timing, in any event, is crucial, and whether you are launching a product or a service, to prepare and announce the launch and then have to postpone it is a mistake – and one that is usually unnecessary and avoidable.

You may need professional help in the launch of your product. If so:

- Do you have the necessary expertise within your own organisation? If so, harness it.
- If you are to use internal resources, make sure that you put in your bid and booking ahead of your internal competitors, who may have simultaneous uses for them. (You regard their intentions as less important than your own, but they may not share your intelligent perspective!)

- If your internal expertise is either non-existent or insufficient, consider outside help, such as public relations consultants and organisations, who can take on anything or everything, from the drafting and layout of a pamphlet or brochure, to the masterminding and administration of the entire launch; or individual consultants or experts, able to deal with specific aspects of the launch, whose efforts your team will co-ordinate.

Whether you are operating wholly or in part through internal or external resources, remember to cost out your launch. It is part of the price of your product or service.

Launching a service

If you launch a new service – either on its own, or alongside, or tied to, a new product, eg, installation, repair or maintenance, adapt and apply precisely the same presentational skills. As services are by their nature often more difficult to describe, in words or in pictures, take special care in their conception and visualising.

37 Conferences and seminars

Business and professional people are often dragooned, shamed or enticed into presenting themselves and their wares at conferences or seminars. To this also there is an art.

Your approach to success depends upon the purpose of the occasion. Is yours, for instance, a promotional exercise, designed to introduce new clients or to strengthen the loyalty of old ones? Do delegates come to learn, from those who are trained and qualified to teach?

Either way, you are in show business. There is no excuse for a dreary conference. However dull the subject, it can be enlivened by visual aids (see Part II); relaxed by wit; brought to life by enthusiasm.

Individual speakers should follow the rules of presentation (Parts I and V). In particular, they should know and prepare their materials; communicate with and according to their audiences; speak with style and demonstrate with skill.

Whether dealing with a small-scale teaching seminar or a larger assembly or conference, excellent presenters respect their audiences and entertain them. The fact that so many conferences are dull and disastrous is a denunciation of those who organise and address them. They harm not only their own cause, but they also spoil the market. They forget that while schoolchildren are tied to their desks and to their classrooms, conference delegates can opt for the bar, and today's seminar attenders will be tomorrow's absentees. Hence the disease of 'conference syncopation' – staggering from bar to bar!

Presenters' success depends to a vast extent on the conditions created for them by the conference or seminar organisers. Check these in advance, preferably before you agree to take part. If, for instance, the room is to be vast and the audience small, the acoustics echoing and the amplification minimal, the delegates crowded and unhappy, and the food inedible – then do not attach your good name to their bad feelings. Also, remember to order any visual aids or other necessary equipment.

In any event, arrive early enough to check your atmosphere and your apparatus, your audience and your audibility. Pay special regard to the following:

- Is the stage, platform and/or table as you like or need it?
- Stuck as *you* are with the amplification arrangements as *they* are, how can you make the best of them? For instance, will you be able to remove, adjust and/or stroll with the microphone, or is it fixed?
- Is the overhead projector or other equipment for your visual aids in proper order and position? If you need assistance in, perhaps, the showing of slides, is it available?
- If you need particular arrangements for your comfort and convenience, will you get them? These may range from water for a dry throat, to (in my case) somewhere quiet for a lunchtime nap and battery recharge. The same applies to the provision of pre-meal drinks or intermission tea or coffee.
- If you are to be paid a fee for your presentation, are the arrangements clear, recorded or confirmed in writing and followed through? If these are to any extent on a commission, bonus or other arrangement that depends upon the success of the event, then how will you find out what you are owed; and will you need to send an account or invoice?
- Should you require smokers to remain at the back or to one side, or will you mix the chimneys with the abstainers? Or can you prohibit smoking?
- Always try to fill up seats from the front. If you are not sure whether the room will be filled, try to make sure that no one sits in the back rows until front and centre are full.
- If you are to be introduced by a Chair or other impresario, has he or she adequate and correct details for the purpose? Have you arranged for details, samples or goods – or order forms, brochures or other documents – to be properly and prominently displayed?
- Try to avoid interruptions from the clatter of crockery and cutlery, before and after breaks. Separate reception and coffee rooms will help, but thin partitions destroy the best of plans.

Prepare for a climax at the end, so that your delegates/audience leave happy. If you cannot manage flowers for the women, then at least ensure applause for your speakers.

38 Meals and banquets*

Presentations *at* meals and banquets are even more perilous than after-dinner speeches. All the usual presentational rules apply, with sharpened emphasis. For instance:

- Study the size, shape and likely atmosphere of the venue, before you decide on the best type of presentation and (in particular) on your visual aids.
- The size of the hall should not affect the sound of your amplified voice – but the greater the space, the larger the visual aids required. If, for instance, you wish to use video or similar equipment, will you need special projectors and wider screens? Will you hire them? If so, at what cost and will it be justified?
- As a mealtime presenter, you join the ranks of the cabaret artiste. Ask successful performers in that most complex craft and they will explain the pitfalls. For instance, instead of having your audience in front of you, with their bodies and their heads hopefully turned in your direction, they will be scattered and clumped around tables, eyes and minds concentrated on plates and glasses. Some may turn their heads, their bodies, or even their chairs, so as to watch you. Others will allow your voice to go in one ear and out the other, without allowing their eyesight to interfere with their hearing.

So, keep the lights on, your presentation lively and varied. If possible, use a roving microphone. Place yourself wherever most people can see you with least discomfort – whether that be at the front, at the side, or in the middle. If there is a platform – for the band or for the top table – use it. If there is none, and you want one, ask for one.

If you use a microphone, remember that there is no law that confines you to your own seat or table. If that would place you with your back to the audience, switch places with someone opposite, or stand in the best position.

If possible, work out your routine beforehand and co-ordinate arrangements with the Master of Ceremonies, the *maitre d'*, the impresario, Chair or toastmaster. Above all, do not underestimate your massive task. The standard presentation is tough enough – the mealtime misery is best summed up by the remark attributed to the prophet Daniel: 'At least when they threw me into the lions' den, I

---

* See also Chapter 25 – Words for Occasions.

knew that I wouldn't be required to make a presentation when the ghastly meal was over!'

If you *organise* a mealtime occasion to be preceded or followed by a presentation, please bear the presenter's problems most carefully in mind. Indeed, if you are the provider of the banquet, check in advance how best to ease the presenter's task. Use the above notes as a checklist and then consider the following:

- As with all gatherings, a few people packed into a small room should help to produce success; but a large audience half filling a vast area is the surest guarantee of failure. If in doubt, pack them in. If necessary, use partitions.
- Select your top targets and ensure that they are well seated. If in doubt about their preferences, enquire: 'Would you prefer to be at the top table or with the French Ambassador/Board of Directors (or as the case may be)?' Human dignity is never more vulnerable than when its bearers are on public view. Those who consider themselves separated from the great – either by too great a distance or at all – may leave before the presentation begins. Or if they are physically present, their minds will be concentrated on revenge.
- If you must have a top table, then perhaps it should be a round one, in the centre of the room, so that far more people may feel that they are close to it. Or maybe you could put your speakers or presenters on one side of the main table, with sprigs stretching out from it – and top colleagues hosting from the far end of each sprig? Or a director to host each table?
- Beware of rushing. Allow for those without whom you cannot sit down to be reasonably late – then insist that the banquet begins as near as possible to the precisely planned minute.
- If time is short and the presentation crucial, use guile to reduce the time taken by the meal. Did you know that you can cut meal times by about ten minutes if you serve fish or meat *off* the bone, rather than leaving your guests to fiddle for ages with, for instance, the carcass of a capon or a calf? You could also serve the coffee immediately after the main course together with the dessert?
- Consider breaking up the presentation. For instance, maybe someone should speak to your guests before the meal – but be careful with this one. I once attended an Indian banquet with 12 speeches before the meal was served. Nor was our mood improved by the extreme heat of the Madras curry that followed!

At luncheon meetings at which I present an organisation to important guests, I always introduce the guests to the organisation between the main course and the desert. Then I tell our guests about us. That leaves time after coffee is served to introduce, hear and then thank our guest speaker.

In Belgium, I addressed a dinner at which there were four speeches between the main course and the dessert. I was the last. I enjoyed misquoting the famous and prophetic words of Madame de Pompadour, who had said: '*Après nous le déluge*' – after us will come the deluge. I said with apparent truth: '*Après moi le dessert*' – the audience got their desserts as quickly and as sweetly as I could put across my message.

Mealtimes may be for messages – but wise presenters and their hosts ensure that the length of the speeches and presentations is in inverse ratio to the magnificence of the meals.

39   Close-up contacts and individual planning

The most sensitive presentations are those made individually, personally and close-up. You may feel uncomfortable if you try to sell on an aircraft, but comfort in times of sharp competition is an outdated luxury. So consider the presentation to the close-up contact, wherever found.

Magic is a universal art, whether performed from afar or close-up. But the skills for close-up artists are different, in style and in presentation. So it is with other presentations. When your prospect is alongside you, then the approach is more subtle, and less expansive, direct or aggressive.

How, then, should you operate 'close-up' to your actual or potential clients? Here are some suggestions:

- To strike up a relationship with fellow travellers, and to turn acquaintances into friends, look for their interests. They may advertise these through tie, badge, luggage labels, the obvious contents of hand luggage, or the correspondence that you cannot help seeing because the victim lays it out before you – if not deliberately, at least with no attempt to hide it.
- Your company should pay for first, business, executive or club class travel for your comfort, but also because you will share it with others at your commercial level. So will those of your fellow travellers – if they may be prospects for you, so you may be for them. Mutual curiosity has promoted many a joint business venture.
- The interests of worthwhile contacts will include their business or professional concerns. So once you have enquired about theirs, they may reasonably ask about yours. Your questions will have begun as innocently as comments about the weather and will shade from one subject into the next.
- If your approaches go wrong, you can always shrug and switch off. The Soviet Union was once compared to an aircraft because its routine is well ordered; it sometimes makes you feel sick; and once you are in, it is not so easy to get out. Emerging from an aircraft conversation can usually be achieved with a sigh and a murmur that it is time to sleep. Saying 'I must get some work done, I'm afraid' may be even an indication of diligence, making you worthy of some future fee.
- Always carry business cards, especially in Japan and the East. A smart and

101

legible business card is essential to courteous introduction and to future contact. An exchange of cards is an invitation to keep in touch. Give generously and collect avidly.

- It may be undignified to ask for work, but it is far more so to be unable to pay your debts – or to be unemployed. Casual contacts will not resent being turned into customers or clients, provided that they get value for money.
- Mealtimes are best for chatting – one thread of conversation may easily weave into the cloth of commerce.
- Like seeks like and trades with it. So obviously the more likeable you appear and the more mutually interesting your ventures, the more joint they are likely to become.
- The golf club – including the 19th hole – is an obvious source for contacts.
- I once asked a distinguished statesman how it was that he maintained such happy personal friendships with so many rulers, in so many diverse places. He replied: 'Because I talk family, music, theatre, sport . . . and then turn to politics. The personal word leads to the political as well as to the personal friendship – and the transfer of this worthy tactic of politics to business is entirely appropriate.
- You may begin by selling *to* your prospects – and end by buying *from* them. Good luck to you both.

40   Appeals and fund-raising

The art of charitable fund-raising involves presentations at many levels. Before you agree to become Chair, treasurer, or even an active member of a fund-raising committee, consider whether you are prepared to accept involvement on a far more time-consuming scale than those who attempt to seduce you into their net would admit. Better to say 'no' now than to opt out in mid-failure.

If you do accept, do not place too much faith in professional fund-raisers. They may help you to structure your efforts by creating an office, files, accounts and the like. They may also advise you on basic techniques, like casting your net for the big fish first. But there is no substitute for your own devotion, emotion and promotion, motivated both by your enthusiasm for the cause and your unwillingness to fail.

Before you even decide on the nature of your fund-raising presentation, you must target the individual – personal or corporate. Once you have your base, you can work from it.

By all means honour your top donors with appropriate positions of distinction – you may say 'thank you' to those whose actual or promised generosity will ensure the success of your appeal.

For a presentation to be appealing, it must have direct and personal relevance to the victims. The wealthier the recipients or listeners, and the greater their reputation for generosity, the more appeals they will receive. Benevolent millionaires have told me that they get anything up to 200 appeal letters a week. Most of the 'round robins' are consigned to the basket. The vast bulk of replies must say 'No'. The ones that produce results are almost invariably those from people whom the would-be donors feel that they should not disappoint, and for causes well-presented. At best, the ready response results from altruistic benevolence – the cause is worthy and the giver willing.

Self-interest often plays its part. The best 'prospect' for the heart foundation is the businessman with cardiac disease. The softest touch for the home for backward children is the parent of a mentally handicapped child. Those who give to a trade benevolent association may wonder whether, one day, they may need its help – or may be grateful that they do not.

Self-interest takes other forms, too. Some people like to leave a touch of immortality for themselves or their families through the naming of a building or a bed, or an inscription in a book, or on a roll of honour. Honour – approval, popularity, dignity, appreciation – and through them, perhaps, power.

Then there is money. Everyone in business knows that to earn you must spend. You may also ask associates to follow your generous lead. Call it sordid blackmail if you like, but when the chairman of your main customer company asks for a donation for his pet charity, can you refuse? Anyway, you have your pet project, haven't you? The day will come when you will write to the person who raided your pocket, saying: 'I am sorry to be a nuisance, but the cause is excellent.' He or she will sigh, and return the compliment which you paid in the past. The cynic may have little use for either of you, but the organisers of the charity and (far more important) its beneficiaries, will bless you both.

We all want blessings. The doing of good deeds and charitable giving lie at the root of every religion – and even those who are irreligious may respond to non-secular appeals, just in case.

So successful appeal-makers have much in common with the salesman. They must study their market and frame and angle their letters and speeches accordingly. All have their own methods. Study those of the successful – and copy them. Before you criticise, consider the results.

A famous beggar is said to have approached a leading Rothschild. 'Will you help me?' he asked.

'You know that I do my best not to refuse help,' replied the charitable magnate. 'But I really do feel that when you come to see me, you might at least wear clean and respectable clothing.'

The man looked down at his shabby garb and then up at his prospective benefactor. 'Mr. Rothschild,' he said gently, 'Do I presume to tell you how to run your bank? No. Then please do not tell me how to beg!'

So learn from others. Make a collection of the appeal letters, brochures and circulars that you receive, and ask yourself, 'Which ones strike home to me? Which have meaning and vitality? Which make me pay?' When you know that, your research is becoming productive.

Usually, you will find that the letters which are really appealing have sincerity, simplicity and personality as their keynotes. Their presentation is sufficiently unusual to remove them from the ruck.

And the ones that really matter will be enclosed with a personal note.
Three more rules are:

- Remember that the best fund-raisers are those who give – of themselves and of their money. They win by example.
- Ask the recipients of your appeal to respond to you personally – so that they do not think they will escape by sending a few pennies to some impersonal appeals organiser.
- If yours is a charity, make sure that it is registered; that you include its registration number; and that you give the option of convenants.

Collecting money for charity is big business, highly competitive, and requires the best organisation to produce even reasonable results.

A word from the head of a very generous charitable foundation: 'When I receive beautiful brochures on splendid art paper, I get cross, and the charity generally gets nothing from me. If it has that sort of money to throw away, then it cannot be as short of funds as it says.' The converse, from a rival philanthropist: 'You must spend money to raise money. Unless you have a good-looking, well produced and professional set of literature, I will not believe that you are a well and professionally run charitable organisation in which I should invest.'

There must be a happy medium somewhere – find it.

41   Your message

The purpose of a presentation should be clear from beginning to end. The start sets the tone; the finish decides whether the message or the presenter gets carried away. Far too many presentations simply fade into anti-climax. As the last sentence droops to its end, the speaker says: 'Thank you' and collapses gratefully back into his seat. The key questions you must consider if your message is to get through are:

- What is your message?
- Who will convey it?
- Where – venue and atmosphere?
- When – timing?
- How? And above all,
- What do your audience want?

Your conclusion and your message should emerge from your final sentence – with your voice and your audience uplifted. Not to give the message at the end of your presentation is like going fishing and casting an unbaited hook into the water.

So work out your message in advance; spell it out from your early words; and leave it well sunk into your audience as you depart. Nothing so becomes a good presentation as an excellent conclusion. Nothing so destroys it as a sentence without end, an end without message. End *up* – with a climax. Not with a limp 'thank you.' Pause. Lift up your voice and your audience will leave uplifted.

PART VI

Techniques and teams

42 The art of introduction

There is one absolutely sure way to make almost anyone in public life hate you for the rest of his and yours. Go up to someone and say: 'You don't remember me, do you?' When he or she replies: 'Of course I do. How are you?', then retort: 'If you remember me, tell me where we met and what my name is'.

If he is a statesman, he may then reply: 'I'm sorry, but your name escapes me at the moment.' If he is a mere politician – especially an MP with a very large majority – he may say what he thinks, which is: 'If ever I did know your name, I am pleased that I have forgotten it!'

To make or keep friends, and to influence others, present yourself to anyone who may conceivably have forgotten who you are by saying: 'I am John Brown' (assuming that that is your name).

I once hosted a reception for the Queen. I steered the great lady down a corridor between ranks of admiring subjects, each attempting the impossible task of pressing forward so as to be as near as possible to Her Majesty and hopefully to be presented to her, whilst at the same time being courteous and kindly and pressing backwards, if only to hold back those who were pressing forwards.

At the end of her apparent ordeal, I said: 'Your job must be extremely difficult, Ma'am.'

'Not really,' she replied. 'You see, I so rarely have to introduce myself!'

If you are 'presented' to the Queen or any other greatness, others will introduce you. Find out in advance the correct form of address. With the Queen it is, 'Your Majesty', and thereafter 'Ma'am'. Ladies still curtsey and men bow, but the inclination of knee or head is far less pronounced than in more courtly days. And those who forget seldom end up in the Tower of London.

Still, for anyone seeking self-preservation or self-advancement, self-presentation is a worthwhile art.

What then of the presentation of others? Face to face and in theory, you present the lesser to the more distinguished. For example, 'Good morning, Chairman. May I introduce our new branch manager?' Conversely, the managing director of potential clients would get introduced to your top man thus: 'Mr Haikoda, may I introduce you to our chairman, Mr Martin Green?'

Public introductions require far greater care and skill than most executives are prepared to give them. Most introductions are sloppy and inadequate and some are downright insulting.

The first and ultimate disaster is to forget your guest's name. The most infamous example was the chairwoman who introduced Edward Heath to a 1970 election audience. 'Fellow Conservatives,' she said, 'it is my privilege to introduce to you a man whose name is a household word . . . our next Prime Minister . . . Mr. . . .' And then, to the misery of her audience, but to the absolute delight of millions of television viewers, she forgot. The next PM (as indeed he was) glowered impassively. She did not become a Dame.

So write down the names of your guests, even if they are your closest friends – which they will cease to be, if you forget their names in the private panic of the public moment.

The second disaster is by far the most common: 'Our guest tonight is far too well known to require any introduction . . .' Roughly translated, that means: 'I have been too lazy to find out anything about him. Indeed, I have not even bothered to ask him what he would like me to say in his introduction.'

The better known your guest, the more delighted the audience will be to hear some unexpected anecdote, some illustration of prowess, some clue from the past to the eminence of the present, and the reason for his or her presence.

The third misery is the presenter who introduces speakers by usurping their speeches. Touch on the subject for the occasion; but it is not for you as host, Chair or impresario to give the talk, the lecture or the analysis. If you had been invited to give the serenade, you would have been asked to bring your violin.

A public introduction should take the form of a mini-speech, with a sensible opening; a structured whole; and a climactic ending: 'Ladies and Gentlemen, Mr . . . Victor . . . White . . .'

When introducing a guest, you can sometimes say too much. For instance, if there is only one person alongside you, you do not need to say: 'On my left, I have Mr. . . .'

If *you* are introduced in public, listen carefully to the introduction. With any luck, it will provide your immediate, topical and light-hearted lead-in to your own speech – an ice-breaker to create the rapport that you need with your audience. Here are some standard winners:

- After the fulsome, overgenerous and probably overlong *cv*: 'I do thank you, Mr. Jones, for that magnificent obituary!' Or,
- 'After that introduction, I can scarcely wait to hear myself speak.' Or,
- 'These days, no managing director' (or chairman, scrap dealer, as the case may be) 'can afford to turn away any compliment, however undeserved. So I thank you for your introduction.'

If you are faced with the opposite – the non-existent, needs-no-introduction, non-presentation – simply introduce yourself. Explain why you are happy to address this particular audience. And with that obvious modesty for which all top people are so justly renowned, hint gently at the reasons why your audience are so privileged to have you as their guest, even if the host who preceded you failed in his or her task. If the introduction came to a bad end, one way or another, it should provide you with a useful beginning.

43   The lost art of the interview

Employers expect to acquire the art of interviewing by instinct and to perform it by intuition. Result: catastrophic decisions – or, sometimes, correct choices with expensively selected candidates rejecting jobs offered.

So what are the basic rules for successul interviewing? How can you best assess interviewees – their present, their past, their personality, and their views and talents. How can you judge whether they will fit into your team or (on occasion) whether they should stay there or be promoted, demoted or moved sideways? How do you present your own or your company's image, or both?

Some business interviewers regard themselves as part-time agents of the KGB. Neither personal nor industrial relations are branches of the martial arts. The more miserable you make your interviewees, the less you find out about them. They do not need your help to create their stress. You should make victims welcome. Begrudge not your smile. Explain the purpose of the occasion – a little about the company, the organisation, the team, the requirements and yourself. Then pass the ball to them.

Most interviewees are most fluent when talking about that which interests them most – themselves. So ask about the interviewee's interests. Use *cv*s as a lead-in – prod, gently. Help them to reveal that which they wish to hide. Percolated kindness is a far better weapon for the interview than thoughtless cruelty. Isn't your purpose to entice your victims out of their shell? Then avoid anything that will send them back in. You wish to remove the barriers between you? Then do not sit on one side of your desk with them on the other.

Plan the operation. As a leading politician once remarked: 'If you do not know where you are going, you will probably end up somewhere else!'

The formality of form filling destroys the informality of the successful interview. So get your victims to fill in forms beforehand –and complete yours after they leave. But do not overplan – a good interview finds its own momentum and runs its individual course.

An interview session is a two-way assessment and (in general) the kinder and the more relaxed its path, the more appropriate its ending. As the dentist said to his patient, 'Now, we're not going to hurt each other, are we?'

Assess the interviewees on the basis of their potential, as reflected by records. Look especially for undeveloped talents. Remember the tale of the millionaire who caught a burglar in his garden with a transistor radio in his pocket. The police said to the tycoon: 'What do you want us to do with him?' 'Let him go,' answered the millionaire, 'We all started small!'

You are dealing with supplicant human beings who may want your job more than they are prepared to show. A judge described a company as having 'no body to be burned, no soul to be damned'. Your interviewee has both – and tomorrow you may be on the other side of the table, so be kind. To select the wrong candidate is an expensive and wasteful irritation, and to have the right one reject you is even worse.

The clerk to a court once asked an accused: 'Are you guilty or not guilty?' He replied: 'If you don't know, why should I tell you?'

Ask the questions that you need answered; and invite the interviewee to return the compliment. Above all, listen. God gave man two ears and one mouth so that we might listen twice as much as we speak. Interviewers who listen will not only improve their judgment, but also impress interviewees by making them feel that they have had a fair hearing. If they win the job, they are more likely to want it; if they lose, then they are less likely to blame you.

Try to avoid unnecessary interviews. The larger the likely response to your advertisement or job invitation, the greater the need for a clear and precise specification. The more specific and known your aim, the fewer your targets. If your interviews are many, each victim should bring a mugshot, since the greater the list, the more unsure the memory.

Choose interviewers and interviewees with equal care. Listen with concentration and consideration. Then, with luck, your decision will be acceptable to your chosen one in the short term, and to you in the test of commercial time.

Finally, never forget that when you carry out an interview, you are also yourself being interviewed. Too many businesses spend too much money on choosing the right people for jobs, only to have themselves turned down. So when dealing with interviewees, present the job on offer as one worth doing. If either you or the job appear to be boring, you cannot expect much interest from the best applicants.

Even in awful days of high recession, the few who are chosen may also choose.

44   Groups, teams and delegations

A group or team presentation is more difficult than one made by an individual. Functions are divided and faults multiplied. The success of a presentation made by a group or delegation depends first on discipline and leadership.

Not long ago, I joined an international delegation calling on the President of an East European state – a man of huge power. He had, we were told, allocated one hour to see us, so we arranged that one of the group who spoke the host's language would briefly introduce the rest of us and the subjects for discussion. We would then listen with the sharpest attention to our host's response. We filed into the room and were duly greeted and seated. Some 55 minutes later, my colleagues paused to take breath and our host was allowed to speak!

I had sat quietly fuming. The others could not resist the chance to harangue the mighty – some had even brought prepared word-for-precious-word orations. It was a senseless performance.

Happily, our host was master not only of his nation, but also of his own time: he gave back as good as he got. One hour later, he stopped speaking. In fairness to all, every word was echoed in translation and the entire process took double time. Still, that should have been taken into prior account and actual consideration.

So the first essential for a successful delegation is – discipline. If self-discipline is (as often) at a premium, then it must be enforced by the leader. For the purpose of the delegation, he or she is the Chair of the side; makes the introduction; calls on and calls off the speakers; tries to give each person an opportunity to report back and guides the discussion. The rules on chairing (Part IV) all apply.

Preparation is essential. You must define the object of the exercise and how it may best be achieved. As with any other campaign, you must look out not only for your own tactics but for those of your hosts. How do they react to this approach or to that one? How do you best influence them? Members of your hosts' staff are ideal providers of incidental intelligence about their boss. Can you check them out in advance? Or maybe you can do some on-the-spot sleuthing?

Edward Heath received a delegation at 10 Downing Street. We were early; he was late. One of his aides was assigned to keep us happy. I asked him, 'What sort of approaches does the PM like – and dislike?'

'With him,' came the prompt reply, 'you use an argument once. If he rejects it, find another one. He is impatient with repetition.'

One-person delegations are best. Unless you need backing – the full weight of personality and experience or a supplement to your own knowledge – go alone if you can. The greater numbers, the less chance that your hosts will unwind. As an experienced lobbyist explained: 'A delegation is like a committee. It should always consist of an odd number. And three is too many.'

But if the pressures from those who have a *right* to be there (in their own minds or in yours), whom you accept willingly, or because you do not wish to cause them offence, forces you into an unwieldy number, try to hack it down by blaming your hosts – 'They are only prepared to receive half a dozen of us . . .'

Insist upon discipline of speech. Appoint a spokesperson or accept that role for yourself. The larger the party, the greater the preparation and discipline required. If possible, choose your colleagues so that each can fire different arguments.

A two-person business presentation is often best when one takes the soft, kindly and friendly line while the other puts in the boot. So in the larger-scale approach, vary the diet and the attack, according to the personalities and the prospects.

Share out the subjects or material between you. Approach the client, the customer and the presentation from different angles so that you plough the field from different directions. Each of you should deal with your own area of expertise, your own specialised angle.

Plan in advance how to avoid repetition and overemphasis leading to boredom; or leaving out essential information or arguments – leading to failure or defeat.

Refer back to what was said by a previous speaker – 'As my colleague has pointed out . . .' Or, 'Now let me elaborate on/present a different aspect of the suggestion made by . . .' Also, refer forward to future remarks – 'My colleague, Mrs Jones, will deal with/explain this in detail . . .'

Find out how your host or prime prospect likes to be addressed, and oblige. Mighty personages prefer to be called by the name of their office as a tribute to their success; lesser achievers may have an even greater need for dignity. Ambassadors and Foreign Heads of State should be addressed as 'Minister', 'Chairman', 'President', 'Sir', or 'Your Excellency'.

45   In attendance

Whether in business, politics, or diplomacy, delegations and other teams of presenters or lobbyists often bring an executive, secretary or personal assistant. He or she services the board or team, and acts as their convener, secretary, memory and scribe.

I once led a delegation to see Prime Minister Thatcher. With us came the General Secretary of the organisation, who sat with pencil poised.

'I thought this was a private session,' said the PM, fixing the poor man with a stern eye. 'Off the record, informal.'

Our colleague speedily got rid of the offending items. The meeting had not begun well.

So always ask yourself:

- Is it or is it not an occasion when you need to have officials 'in attendance'?
- If yes, what part, if any, should they play during the actual presentation?
- Should they 'take a note' during the proceedings – or make one after the meeting, to revive, refresh and record what happened?
- Should they stay behind, after the session concludes, to tie up loose ends, like making arrangements for the next session or for future consultations or communications, or for an agreed press release?

The attendance of an appropriate official may add standing, weight and efficiency to your presentation. But it may also change the tone and colour of the occasion. Use your company secretary, personal assistant, or official right hand to supplement your approaches, but take care to ensure that your aides are properly briefed, so that they know what the occasion and the team will require.

46 Management – top, middle and below

Basic presentational rules in no way differ according to the level of management which is at the giving or receiving end of a presentation. But the lower the level, the more likely it is that presentations will be made *within* the organisation – to more junior managers; to the sales force; to the workforce; to union or staff representatives.

Some rules that are universally applicable need special emphasis for in-house presentations – and there are other specific hints worth remembering. Here is a checklist of some of the most essential:

- Treat staff and workforce with the same respect that you would outsiders. Where appropriate, preserve formalities.
- Know your audience – and get your facts right. They are more likely than strangers to recognise errors.
- Involve and respect your colleagues' own interests – for example, *financial* interests, (ie, let them know how compliance with your exhortations will increase their pay or prospects), and *time* (keep your presentations brief).
- Use visual aids, as you would in any other presentation – and remember, the less sophisticated the audience, the simpler the language should be.
- Keep and use a store of 'funnies' – especially apt illustrations from happenings within the company or organisation.
- Try out your themes and tactics on trusted colleagues before you let yourself loose on others – especially if some of *them* may have control or power over *your* future.
- Treat presentations as part of your on-going communications system – regular or special. Always consider your audience – its status, level and responsibilities.
- Communicate with your listeners – and speak and welcome their participation – as colleagues.
- When dealing with your juniors, talk up, not down.
- Tell your listeners the good news as well as the bad. Resist the temptation to disclose information only when it will assist in reducing pay claims. When sales, production or other results are good, tell them – even before your accountants have salted away the winnings in the tax, staff pension, boiler replacement, or other reserve fund.
- Do not assume that all your colleagues know as much as they should. Start at the beginning – and explain.

118

- Do a professional job on your production, with documents, visual aids and overall presentation. The phrase: 'We are only talking to our own workforce/salesforce/colleagues' should be expunged from the internal presenter's vocabulary.
- Define your objectives, primary and secondary – and limit the points you intend to make. Start with them at the beginning and leave with a message at the end. If there are too many points, reserve the less urgent for next time.
- Speak clearly and audibly.
- Do not damage future relations by putting on an uncharacteristic act – stay in character.
- Above all and again, *know your audience* – its idiosyncracies and even its language. If you are talking to part of your workforce which includes, for instance, some who have limited knowledge of the English language, speak simply – and if necessary, use an interpreter.

My most difficult audience is my own family. The larger the gathering of the clan, the greater the certainty that an error will go down into history, to mellow and improve with time and retelling.

Your colleagues at any level are an enlargement of the tribe. Internal presentations need the same preparation, care, attention and skill as any other, or perhaps even more – external mistakes will fade into the lore of lost contracts, forgotten chances. Clangers, howlers, and errors, made within your own outfit, will live on to your eternal discomfort.

119

47   Training

If you introduce employees to their jobs, consider how best to teach the most in the least time. That will depend, of course, on the nature and complexity of the work, the prior training and skill of the trainees – and their basic intelligence and skill. (Your organisation may, of course, have its own personnel department, skilled in handling and training new recruits.)

Trainees must themselves be trained in basic presentation skills or they cannot hope to reach their own maximum potential. The rules are set out in Parts I and II of this book, but trainers should also remember the following:

- Know your trainees. Study their *cv*s and do not waste training on skills that people already possess; but do not presume knowledge and skill merely because trainees have paper qualifications – start by testing.
- When talking to trainees, follow the suggestions on talking to colleagues, detailed in Chapter 46. In particular, ensure involvement and interest; harness trainees' personal interests; and do not talk down to them – especially if some of them may eventually rise above you.
- Consider in each circumstance whether training documentation should be provided and studied *before* a course on presentation; or while it is going on (either while you are making it or during breaks, including evenings or weekends); and/or kept and read and/or used for reference afterwards. Make sure any documentation intended for reference is properly indexed.
- Remember to provide copies of slides, transparencies, or other visual aids. At best, these should be available during lectures or presentation, so that trainees can use them for marking and/or note taking on, eg, additional explanations.
- Learn from the experts. Attend a variety of courses or conferences, watch how the presenters cope with their audiences, and then adopt, adapt and use those techniques that you particularly admire and that fit in with your own style and purpose. Conversely, ensure than neither you nor your colleague trainers makes the mistakes that you observe and dislike in others.
- When induction training is completed, assess the performance of trainees and discuss it with them. Also consider if, when and how you need follow-up, refresher or up-dating presentations.

48 Radio

Ask any experienced radio producer or interviewer which are the best and which the worst categories of performers and you will almost always get the same answers. The best? Professionals – such as most actors or politicians – and especially politicians because they are used to making up their own scripts as they go along. The worst? Industrialists and business people – closely followed, for different reasons, by academics and teachers – with engineers, technicians and other jargon-ridden and often pedantic experts coming an easy third.

If *you* have to make a radio appearance, how can you avoid joining the ranks of the awful? How can you make the best of this great opportunity, and at the same time maximise your chances of being asked back? Here is your quick guide to successful radio broadcasting.

Victim's choice

Where possible, choose your programme. Know your market and how you are most likely to reach it – and know your interviewers and who is most likely to be helpful.

Often you will have no choice or will simply be grateful for any outlet that you, or your staff or PR people, can find for you. But while beggars may not be choosers, astute victims often can be – you may refuse to appear.

Preparation

The worst interviewees are those who do not know their subject. Most occasional or amateur broadcasters are interviewed, and all interviewers operate, on the adversarial principle (see Chapter 43 on interviewing). Their job is to probe and to seek out facts and opinions. If *you* do not know your facts, you will get no respect for your opinions. (See also Chapter 51 on phone-ins).

Strangely, business people often get bottom marks for knowledge, while being expert within the narrow and limited confines of the subject about which they want to talk. Remember that interviewers place themselves in their listeners' place and look on the broader scene. So if you do not want to get floored by an unexpected question, do your homework, and prepare answers to the questions you least want to answer.

On time

Time on the air is extremely expensive. You may be offered yours free of charge, so do not abuse the hospitality. You will only come late once for a programme, a producer or a radio station. You will not be asked again, nor will they be the least interested in even the best of excuses.

The important of being early is not merely to avoid coming late. It also enables you to settle in, to reduce panic, to chat up the staff and (if possible) your interviewer – and especially to discover the intended main lines of your unscripted contribution.

Hopefully, your interviewer will also be on time. If programmes are going out live, then to be late may cost them their jobs. The difference is that you are in their kingdom.

The ultimate in reporter lateness provided me with one of my few and cherished (but as yet unrealised) chances to enter the Guinness Book of Records. Some years ago, I arrived my customary few minutes early for a local radio recording session. The engineer was there but the reporter was not. Half an hour later, he had still not appeared. I then made my revolutionary suggestion to the man in charge – 'Let me interview myself!' I said. 'I promise to ask myself the nastiest and most probing questions. And you can dub in the reporter's voice when he turns up!'

To my delight, he agreed. I interviewed myself with immaculate courtesy. I dug away at my own weak points, being careful, of course, to provide succinct and appropriate answers. When the interviewer turned up, his questions were duly slotted into place.

Unfortunately, the chances of your being able to ask yourself questions are remote. But if you know in advance the questions that your interviewer is likely to put to you, then you may do almost as well. Ask how long your contributions will last, and do not despise the 60-second plug. Just as one photograph in a newspaper is more effective than ten columns of print, so a minute on the air is worth reams of advertising copy.

The briefer the appearance, however, the more concisely you must make your points. So work out in advance those points that you are determined to make. Slot them into as few sentences as possible. Then be prepared to expand on each, if you are given the chance. Make notes, but (unless you are reading a pre-prepared and timed contribution) do not prepare a word-for-word script. Not only will it sound contrived if you are given the chance to read it, but you will probably have to work without it. And if you are used to leaning on your crutch you will miss it when the interviewer forces you to cast it aside.

Scripts

If you are asked to give a scripted talk, then it will probably have to be timed, if not to the second, then to the 30 seconds. It will require the producer's approval. So have your script typed in double spacing on A4 paper or its equivalent, with plenty of copies. Stick to the theme that you have been given and keep your commercials reasonably subtle. Think about your audience and what the producer wants you to put across to them. Do not allow sentences to run over from page to page, and always end a paragraph and a page together.

When you have prepared your piece, read it out aloud and time it. Remember that you are better off to put less across well than to pack too much into too short a broadcast. Read your script over on to a tape recorder and play it back. Get your wife/husband/children/or your close friends to criticise.

When reading your script, project your eyes and your mind ahead. Be sure to avoid paper rattle. Do not *turn* pages – instead, lift each sheet gently from the pile and place it noiselessly to one side.

Be prepared to amend your script even at the last minute, so as to make it topical. For instance, I broadcasted four early-morning, three-minute religious items – affectionately known as 'God-spots'. Each day, the producer asked me to lead in from current news – terrorist bombs, religious festivals, anti-nuclear demonstrations or whatever was in the headlines. And the programme presenters added their comment at the end, so that each presentation finished with a chat. Even when you are carefully scripted, prepare for flexibility.

123

49   Radio style

Professionals have style – and radio style requires study and practice.
Here are its main elements:

Voice

If you are lucky, you will have a naturally distinctive voice. Margaret
Thatcher, Neil Kinnock, Alistair Cooke, Walter Cronkite, Henry
Kissinger, Robin Day – all of these people can be recognised with
certainty from their first phrase. If *your* voice is unusual, then,
assuming that it is also pleasant to the ear, *retain its individuality.*

If your voice is ordinary, pay special attention to tone and
modulation. Unlike the opera singer, who must reverberate sound,
you can speak as softly as you wish, and leave the engineers to look
after volume.

When you come into the studio, you will be seated in front of a
microphone, firmly placed, or on a table. Your interrogator will sit
opposite. When you are asked, 'Can we have some level, please?',
that is a request to talk. Give your name and position. Your
interviewer may ask a traditionally brilliant question, like 'What did
you have for breakfast?' You can reply with whatever nonsense you
wish. The technician will then adjust your voice level.

Caution: President Reagan was to make a crucial 'state of the
nation' broadcast. The producer said to him: 'Now, Mr President,
please can we have some level. Tell us what you think about our
United States economy?'

'I must tell the nation,' said the President, 'that our economy is in
one hell of a mess!' Unfortunately for him the studio had already
been linked up to loudspeakers in the White House press room.
Despite frantic efforts by the President's advisers, his words were
broadcast around the world, to everyone's delight but theirs.

Concentration

When broadcasting, total concentration is crucial. Distractions abound – faces smile, grimace or simply move behind glass screens; the interviewer sips coffee (gently replacing cup on saucer to avoid any clink or clatter); the hands of the clock move forward. Your attention may start to wander – then comes the unexpected question. You flounder and fail.

The remedy? Concentrate. Allow your mind to move off your subject and you invite disaster – pre-recorded, perhaps, in the privacy of your own home or office, or in a studio, but audible by thousands and inevitably recorded for future transmission. Matters have triumphed over mind, and you will remain in the ranks of the radio amateur until you have learned the broadcaster's most vital lesson – concentrate or lose.

The best help to concentration is posture. Slouch in your chair, sit back and relax, light up a cigarette and let your eyes wander – and you are on your way out. When broadcasting, you have no time to collect your thoughts. They must be poised permanently at the edge of your tongue. The best way to keep them there is to keep your body well forward in your chair – upright and alert.

Concentration may be even more difficult when you are broadcasting 'down the line'. You may be telephoned in your own office and asked to make a statement. If you agree, the process is quick and time-saving. Disconnect any other telephones and hang a 'Do Not Disturb' sign on your door. Prepare for battle.

If the station calling you is modern, the interviewer may simply say: 'Right – I'll just check the level of my machine and we're off.' If it is old, she may say: 'I'll go into the studio and phone you right back. Please keep your line clear.'

Either way, when you start broadcasting – concentrate. Either sit upright in your chair or, if you are a prowler (like me), stand and talk into the receiver. But treat the mouthpiece as if the interviewer's face were appearing above it.

As usual, if the interview is being recorded, don't be afraid of 'fluffs'. 'Sorry,' you say, 'I'll repeat that.' Then do, and leave it to the interviewer or editor to slice out your first and muddled effort. They'll never hold that against you. They have too many miseries of their own to correct, and they are professionals.

Sincerity and brevity

Sincerity is vital. With no sight, only your voice can convey it. Use the same technique as when you are presenting. Understate and, above all, be concise and relevant. Answer the questions you are asked – briefly, accurately and to the questioner's point.

Chat

On the air, talk to the interviewer as though you were having an ordinary chat in a private room with no one else listening. It sounds naturally convincing – and, more important, it helps you. Avoid phrases like: 'I'm sure your listeners will know' or 'those of you out there'. Listeners like to believe that you are broadcasting just to them personally.

Dress and drink

Watch what you wear – for the sound it may make, irrespective of fashion and style. A young woman deafened listeners with a crackling roar every time she breathed because a particularly sensitive directional mike picked up and magnified the sound of her new stiff-fabric bra! It may have done wonders for her figure – but not for her broadcasting. Avoid noisy bangles, beads and leather jackets. And do not 'click' ball point pens or fiddle with paperclips.

Do not drink too much 'hospitality coffee' before committing yourself on air for any length of time. Mother Nature has often destroyed the best of broadcasts. Avoid alcohol. It dulls the keenness of the brain, and on air you need every ounce of it.

50   Anecdote and analogy

Broadcasters who salt their wisdom with wit and pepper their presentations with apt and lively stories and analogies are welcome guests everywhere. Media presentations, after all, are only private conversations writ large and broadcast to the multitudes. So talk to the people in the studio as if they were human – they probably are. Entertain them as you would your friends, and they will not only be friendly but will help you to pass on the good news. Unless you are embedded in the Open University or some other strictly academic emanation, anecdotes and wit are crucial, however brief your talk or interview.

Even academics find their lectures fuller if they strengthen their material with human interest. Humans, after all, need to be interested. And while students at a lecture may be a captive audience, your listeners can switch off – and if you bore them, they will.

51 Phone-ins

The phone-in is the modern hybrid. An inexpensive cross between radio and telephone, it brings the public into the studio and the studio out to the public, at minimal expense and trouble to each. To cope with either as a guest target or as a phoner-in, you must understand what happens in the studio.

The presenter of the programme sits at a table in front of a microphone. The producer sits with the engineer and the telephone operators in a room separated from the live microphones by a barrier of thick glass. The in-coming calls are sifted and sorted. The producer seeks a lively balance from articulate callers while excluding the fanatic, the bore and the loudmouth. Sometimes a technical marvel transmits the caller's words a second or so after they come into the studio, so that foul language and the like may be cut off, if not at source, then before transmission.

Every radio station has its regular callers, some appreciated and others disliked. The best (as usual) present their questions or their case, briefly, knowledgeably and with no waffle. Others get cut off in their prime. They pause to take breath and their voice disappears, by the producer's magical forefinger flick.

Both the programme presenter and the speaker wear their earphones (or 'cans', as they are affectionately known). They hear the incoming call and each other's response.

Phoner and victim alike must know their subjects or take the consequences. How often have *you* cringed at the phoner presenting *your* case with such ignorance that you wish that you were on the other side? Whether you are phoning in or answering back, you must know your case and put it as succinctly as possible. If you are on the attack, the briefer the question and the more vulnerable the target, the more likely you are to draw blood. Conversely, you must parry the thrust with courtesy and, where necessary, with cunning. Like a speaker on a platform, you are always at an advantage. Your only real danger comes from the programme's presenters. If they press an unfair advantage, then you could be in trouble.

Happily, as in the case of any other radio interview (Chapter 51), the interviewer is anxious to produce a lively result and to avoid the miseries of an interviewee drying up. Unlike the pre-recorded epic, the phone-in goes out live and a good interviewer knows what questions to put or to repeat and how to stir the victim into saying as much (where appropriate) as judiciously as possible.

As a victim, watch your words. Talk to your interviewer and forget your (hopefully) thousands of invisible listeners. But never forget that a word out of place is amplified into massive danger. Defamation by radio is libellous – and while the presenter and the radio station are no doubt insured against libel, you are almost certainly not. (Read Chapter 70 and take care whom and how you criticise.) Attack ideas and you are engaged in 'fair comment on a matter of public interest', however unfair your criticism may be. But attack an individual 'so as to lower him in the eyes of right-thinking people' and you are at peril from the law.

The presenter's job is to loosen the victim's tongue. The looser it becomes the better the result – but the greater the danger both for guest and cause. It follows, of course, that you should not drink alcohol, or any other artificial tongue-loosener before going on air. Treat a phone-in with respect. It is as great a trap for the unwary as it is a challenge, an opportunity and a delight for those who know how to use it.

Here are some hints for phone-in presentations:

- When preparing any sort of campaign, always consider using local or national phone-ins for your purposes – including the organisation of calls by colleagues, comrades or fellow campaigners who know what they are talking about.
- If you are yourself a guest, no harm can be done by pre-warning people on your side so that you give the station at least the opportunity to balance the attacks on you and your case by calls from some friendly supporters.
- If you phone in, switch off your own radio. You cannot both talk by telephone and listen to yourself talking at the same time. If you want to be recorded, either for later listening so as to do better next time, or for your family or posterity, get someone else to operate a tape recorder from somewhere else, or operate a machine on which you can record while the sound is off.
- If an opponent is to be a victim, arrange for well-informed and intelligent people to put difficult questions, especially during peak listening time.
- If you are phoning in, be patient – until the number rings and is answered – first come, first served is the general rule. Once you talk to the producer, do not announce that you are 'phoning to reinforce what has already been said'. The object of a phone-in is to get on it and then to stay on, until you have made your point as pungently as possible. Know the ropes and you can get under them.

- If you are a guest, bring a pen. Your hosts will provide paper. Write down the name of the questioner and use it. As the questioner talks, jot down the main points. As you answer them, tick or cross them off. . . the knowledge that the main points are before you will put panic behind you.

A radio station will usually telephone you back to put you on air. You will then be asked to turn off the radio and come back to the phone. Do not go away from the phone again. If you leave it, you can be sure that this will be the precise moment that the programme presenter comes to you. Your chance will be gone – an embarrassing brief silence – a comment of apology from the presenter – and on to the next caller. The best of calls are lost without a word being said and all because the door bell rang.

52 Television – your head on the box

Television is every other sort of presentation, writ large. It is the ultimate challenge for the presenter, with, generally, a maximum potential for exploitation and error alike. Most of the rules and advice already given for radio apply equally to TV. But we now add to sound the dimension of sight. Presentational stakes pile high.

For a start, consider the value of every second – and cherish it. Compare the cost of buying, say, ten seconds on commercial radio as opposed to the same period on TV. The cost of television – in terms of production as well as the price when sold – reflects its potential power and impact.

The oblong screen concentrates, condenses and makes visible (literally) every peril in radio presentation. So use and adapt my radio advice but add new rules required by vision. I repeat: *If you are studying the rules for television, do not start reading at this point in the book*. 'In the beginning,' says Genesis, 'God created the heaven and the earth.' Every good result starts at the beginning.

So turn back to the radio advice, and read (or re-read) it before moving on.

53 Make-up, clothing and grooming

Sometimes, you can go on camera in all your natural beauty. For an outside broadcast, you may have time to brush your hair or to adjust your tie or your scarf, but viewers will see your true complexion. In many small studios that feed material into a TV centre, the victim is not even offered a comb.

But if you perform in a national or regional TV centre, you will be shipped off to the make-up room, either directly or after a rehearsal. Lie back and enjoy it. Someone is bound to say to you afterwards: 'You looked much healthier on the box!' – and so you did. The make-up person can perform cosmetic wonders.

If you are fortunately featured, the make-up genius will be content with 'browning' your complexion. If you do not like the result, complain. The make-up person is trying to please – primarily, his or her own employers, but at least secondarily the sitter. So if, for instance, your hair is combed backwards and you would like it sideways, either ask for a readjustment or grab the brush.

Once the make-up is complete, leave it alone. Try not to blow your nose or your handkerchief will emerge pink and powdered. Leave your face alone.

Remember to adjust your clothes before leaving the make-up room. An unzipped front below the belt is unlikely to show and if it does some kindly soul will warn you. But an upturned collar, an unknotted tie or an open shirt or blouse will make you look slovenly on the screen.

The most minor blemishes are magnified by the screen. The crooked tie, the white label sticking out from the back of the dark blue jacket, dandruff on the shoulder – they will all look ten times worse on screen.

Some studios have wardrobes, but you should nevertheless arrive appropriately dressed. This means:

- In clothing suitable to the image you wish to present; and
- In colours and patterns which will not 'move' or shimmer (or 'strobe') on the screen.

American comedian and interviewer Johnny Carson chooses clothing that changes in pattern under the lights, but *he* can afford deliberate eccentricity. *You* cannot, so here are the basic rules on dress:

- Avoid checks or narrow stripes on suits, ties and (especially) dresses. Medium-dark suits or dresses are best. Keep jewellery simple and not 'flashy', in either sense of that word.
- Avoid black and white. The best colours for shirts are pastel. Do not leave a handkerchief protruding from your pocket – it distracts from your words.
- Put, and keep, a comb or brush in your pocket or handbag.
- Pull down the back of your jacket. Rucking of the collar is ugly.
  Tip: stand up; button the front of your jacket and pull down the back; sit down; then unbutton – your jacket will be in perfect position.

Features and gestures

Your face may be your fortune, but put it on television and it emerges transformed – probably much for the worse. Unfortunately, there is little that you can do about it, other than to relax and hope for the best. Still, here are some suggestions.

Look at the interviewer or at your fellow gladiator, thrown into the same ring for the pleasure of the public. Eye expression is crucial for contact, confidence and conveying sincerity. Believing yourself off screen, you may keep your head still, but surreptitiously swivel your eyes – perhaps for a glimpse of the audience, or the clock, or for a peep at the monitor. Immediately, by chance or by malicious design, the camera switches to you and you look shifty, cunning and wicked. So, keep your eyes on the interviewer or the other speaker.

We all have what we regard as a 'better side' to our face. Use it by all means when posing for photographs. But your tormentors will choose the side for filming, so forget it. It is much worse to appear two-faced than to be viewed from the wrong side. So forget every face other than that of your interviewer or opponent. Ignore lights swivelling or flashing from camera to camera. Concentrate on content – and on keeping still.

The rarer and more sparing the gestures you use, the greater their effect. On TV, every gesture is magnified. The worst offenders are the unconscious scratchers, twitchers, lip-lickers and nose-pickers. But they are followed closely by the wagglers of fingers, the wavers of arms and (even more disastrous) the pounders of fists or the strummers of fingers – which provide not only an awful sight, but also some hideous sound.

Animation should come from your face, especially through your eyes, and from your speech. If either is wooden, your appearance will fossilise. The same commercial giants who are outstanding in their fields may perform badly on the screen.

Be sure to sit up. To slouch on chair or couch may be comfortable and intended to make you look relaxed. It will, in fact, dub you sloppy and unworthy of trust.

If you happen to be one of those unsuccessful performers, at least console yourself with the obverse of the same coin – that some of our greatest, brightest and wittiest professional entertainers are boring in private.

54 Rehearsals

TV rehearsals are a necessary evil. *Necessary* so that directors and producers, floor managers and cameramen, technicians, engineers, masters of sound and of lighting and the rest can get themselves and their apparatus into order. *Evil* because it is often so difficult for victims to remember whether they used their words in rehearsals or 'on the night'.

Your host will decide whether or not to submit you to any and, if so, to what type of rehearsal. Do as he or she tells you. As usual, relax. Leave it to them to get you seated; to provide you with a glass of water; to hang a mike about your neck or to attach it to your clothing; in short to put you and the place into order. Use the time to get yourself acclimatised. Strange surroundings irritate the nerves. Familiarity calms. If you are prepared for rehearsals and use them sensibly, they can help to 'warm you up', which is generally better than going on 'cold'.

A potentially dangerous and insidious form of rehearsal is performed by interviewers. You will want to meet them before the show, if only to break the ice, to check on the line of questioning, and, if possible, to discover the lead-in question. Interviewers will want to check out their quarry and to supplement their own knowledge of whatever subject is or may be at issue. If after your blood, they will also use the occasion for a foretaste, probably for your weaknesses – while lulling you into an undue sense of security, inviting confidences, and putting you off your guard. (Unless they are on your side – which, somehow, never seems to be the case.) So be cautious. If you think you may be in trouble, use your ultimate weapon – and threaten to dry up.

When interviewers have to cope with nervous victims, they use the rehearsal or run-through to relax the interviewees and to give them confidence. Apart from trying to work out the lie of the land, the outline of the questioning, and the nature of the interview, you should try to steer the rehearsal away from the subject.

Turn the tables on your interviewers by relaxing them – reassuring them that you will never dry up and making them like you and want to help you, rather than fuelling their wish to slit your commercial or professional throat. Treat your interviewers with kindness and they may return the compliment. A little time and tact can pay big dividends.

In a studio, the producer and the interviewer reign supreme. You are their hostage, so handle them with care. When asked what he thought of a particularly distinguished interviewer who was shortly to have his way with me, an experienced colleague once told me: 'When dealing with him, the key lies in two words – *re*spect and *sus*pect!' I did, and the occasion proved more pleasant than *ex*pected. It is a system worth following.

55   Television sight and sound

The best way to learn television techniques is to be trained by experts. Next best: make your presentations in front of a video camera and play back the result. Criticise it with family or friends, then get an expert to explain how to put it right.

Then switch on the television and watch amateurs performing. Also, switch on your own critical faculties, and make notes on successes and failures. Here is a list of 'don'ts' I drew up from a quarter of an hour of watching news interviews.

Don't move from centre screen

An MP fiercely attacking strike action held his head firmly to one side. He seemed to be suffering from arthritis of the neck, if not of the brain.

A distinguished cleric, usually a most relaxed and brilliant TV performer did even worse. 'I have the figures here,' he said – and reached down into his briefcase with such speed that he went totally off screen, to the huge delight of his friendly viewers but to the utter misery of the studio. Stay centre screen – and on it.

Don't relax – the camera never dies

Wise judges watch witnesses when they have left the box. Intelligent cameras flash on and off, red lights blinking (when the light on the camera is on, so are you). When the show is on, control your movements, your gestures and your expressions as well as your words – during every precious second of your air time.

Don't look at the screen – ask for an 'eye-line'

Under no circumstances allow your eyes to wander towards those tantalising, flickering, hypnotising monitor screens. If you wish to see yourself speak, use a mirror or a video recorder, not a monitor.

The most difficult form of TV broadcasting is an excruciating torture inflicted on too many who televise 'down the line'. Suppose, for instance, that you are an expert in a particular area of commerce or industry. You are in London. A startling development occurs in, say, Manchester or Scotland. They invite you first to take an aircraft up North, but when that proves impossible, you are invited into a London studio. Enter and you will be asked to sit in front of a highly original backdrop – like Buckingham Palace or Big Ben. Even if you don't know where you are, your audience will make a shrewd guess.

In front of you, you will find a TV screen. It leaps to life with a delightful mirror image of yourself. Use it to adjust your tie, ensure the absence of dandruff and to comb your hair. Then ask them to switch it off. Otherwise, you will be asked a question by 'the voice' and will look at yourself answering it. Even when that answer is moderately intelligent, you have to be a latter-day Narcissus not to be thrown off your stride.

The alternative is little better. 'The voice' raps out its questions at you and you reply into the thin air ahead. The microphone which carries your voice to the millions is probably clipped to your tie or your shirt.

In 'down the line' radio, you can at least clutch a telephone, or talk into a standing or hanging mike. 'Down the line TV' is the presenter's hell on visible earth. To concentrate like hell is your only hope, but here are a few tips:

- Put a bright object on the spot at which you are meant to look. It attracts your eyes and leaves your mind to cope with the questions.
- Ask whether the studio can arrange for you to see your interviewer on the screen ahead. You may be lucky.
- Above all, ask for an 'eye-line'. They will then tell you where to look, so that when you appear on screen you *appear* to be looking at your interviewer and *not* out into space.

Time

In a TV studio, you should not even have to look at the clock. The studio manager (probably the person who led you to your seat) will stand within view of the interviewer and will relay time signals. When there's one minute left, he will raise the forefinger of his right hand. With half a minute left, he will cross his arms, putting his right hand by his left ear; or he will lay a horizontal finger of one hand across the middle of a vertical finger of his other hand. With about 25 seconds to go, the timer will twirl his right wrist, as if signalling to hurry up. And when he gives the deep-sea diver's danger signal – right hand across throat in cutting motion – that means: Stop!

The best time to dive in with your capture-the-last-word summary is when the 'come to a close' hand windmill signal starts. And if it means interrupting someone else – courteously but firmly – go right ahead. That is all part of TV technique.

Position

If you are small and are faced with a very tall person or *vice versa*, consider how you will both fit onto a television screen. Maybe the smaller should be raised on a box, slope, or sidewalk? If you have size problems and the studio do not know you, tell them in advance.

Projection

To succeed on the screen you must project your personality – radiate relaxation without relaxing, confidence without appearing smug or superior, sincerity without gush. The same qualities, in fact, that apply to personal presentation, but with far greater impact.

So how do you achieve these evidently desirable results? You take your natural ability and add training and practice.

Train to success

To acquire TV success through trial and error is almost impossible. If the trials are gruelling and the errors glaring, you will not get asked back for more practice at viewers' expense. TV techniques need training. The idea that anyone is a 'born performer' and will walk before the cameras with assured success is ridiculous. TV presentations must be studied, learned and practised like all other arts – only more so, because clumsiness and error are so much harder to conceal when projected onto the box. (For more on training, see Chapter 49.)

So why not learn in private? Armed with video camera, operator and a TV set, trainers can often revolutionise the trainee's entire presentation approach and appearance. Victims are recorded performing in circumstances of their choice. The artificiality of the moment substitutes for the stress of the studio and produces equally off-putting results. You will learn how to cope with the media; how to think on your feet or even in that seat – thus correcting your own mistakes, without sharing the horror with the millions who deserve a better fate.

Then, when the time comes for the real television ordeal, at least it will seem familiar. Learned techniques become instinctive and the TV studio will no longer be viewed as a place of torture.

Next time you watch TV, write down for yourself some of the clumsy, irritating, inept or repetitive phrases that so often spoil a presentation. The following are words culled from a typical half-hour magazine programme. Avoid them.

- 'If I may say so . . .'
- 'Do you see?'
- 'To be honest . . .'
- 'To be frank . . .'
- 'To tell you the truth . . .'
- 'One must have regard to the facts, musn't one?'
- 'Actually . . .'
- 'Quite frankly . . .'
- 'You see . . .'
- 'Etc etc. . . .'
- 'Well . . .'
- 'Quite honestly . . .'

Add a few 'ers' and 'ums' and be not surprised if the viewer switches off.

Pre-recording

Too many TV and radio programmes are pre-recorded. They are 'put in the can' and edited. What emerges may be a million miles from your intention. You will not know what happens in advance nor can you correct it in arrear.

The pre-recording of any broadcast creates great dangers to you and to your case. And these are especially acute because the absence of immediate transmission may throw you off your guard and invite a relaxed lack of concentration. So beware!

On the other hand, pre-recording does allow you to get rid of at least some of your major errors, if the producer is prepared to help. Apart from exercising libel, you can reckon that your own input into TV editing will be nil – you are in the cutter's indelicate hands.

Producers of interviews frequently take and retake. So if you are dissatisfied, you can do no possible harm by asking for the same privilege. On TV, you will seldom get it – on pre-recorded radio broadcasts you will seldom fail. The cost of production explains part of the difference, along with ease of editing.

So, given the choice between live and pre-recorded, which should you choose? As a victim, take a chance and go live.

I asked a famous interviewer 'What is the worst mistake that most bad interviewees make on radio or television?'

'They don't answer the questions they are asked,' he replied, without hesitation.

'Who are the witnesses who make the worse impression in court?' I asked a distinguished judge.

'Those who do not answer the questions they are asked,' he replied, without pause.

'Who comes out worst at company interviews?' I asked an experienced director.

'Interviewees who do not answer the questions they are asked,' he answered.

So wherever you are presenting yourself or your case, do please answer exactly what you are asked. Listen to the question; have it repeated if you do not understand it, or if you want some extra time to think; then answer *that* question, not the one you would have liked to hear.

Do not follow the rules of Parliamentary question time, unless (as we shall see shortly) you have no reasonable alternative.

A Cabinet Minister was lost while driving through the country-side. He stopped in a village and wound down his window. 'Where am I, please?' he asked a passer-by.

'You are in your car, sir,' the passer-by replied.

'That,' said the Minister, 'is a perfect Parliamentary answer. It is brief, accurate, and adds nothing whatever to the sum total of human knowledge!'

So try to add a touch of information, a spice of wit or a modicum of common sense, or your presentation is hardly likely to sparkle. But you can always do this by way of addition or rider, like this: 'The answer to your question is . . . but perhaps we could ask a different

question?' Or: 'The answer is yes – but please remember that . . .'
First answer, then add.

56   Coping with confrontation

Nothing is more daunting in prospect, more challenging in reality or more lasting in memory than a broadcast confrontation. Apart from audience interrogation – usually by phone-in (see Chapter 51) or audience participation panel programmes (a rarity for all but the most favoured professional) – confrontation comes in one of two forms:

- Gladiatorial combat between two or more guest victims chosen for their particular differences with the others. Or,
- Battle with interviewers.

Keep cool

You lose control of yourself and of your audience at the same moment. Or reverse the thought and the result is the same: lose command of yourself and you cannot command the argument.

So keep cool under fire. Whether you are faced with a hostile interviewer, an arrogant and nasty opponent, or both, retain your dignity. Become speechless with rage or indignation and your case will go unheard. Start shouting and it is done for – and so are you.

Roman promoters and impresarios staged gladiatorial combats to attract and delight their audiences. The modern equivalent is the broadcast confrontation. Each station, programme, producer and reporter has favourite human sacrifices, some of them to comment with charm, wit or venom on any current topic, others reserved for their speciality.

The invitation invariably comes by telephone. If it comes to me, I go through the preparatory considerations set out in Chapter 65. And on balance I usually accept, for the following overriding reasons:

- I believe in the case which I shall be presenting and consider that presentation necessary.
- With due modesty, I approve of the programme's choice of me as the presenter, when it had so many alternatives (I prefer not to ask or to know

143

how many of these they unsuccessfully approached before reaching me!); and anyway, I like to think that I would do the job well.

- I am a masochist, who would despise himself if he turned down this sort of challenge (and so, actually or potentially, are you – or you would not be reading this chapter).

Once I agree to appear, I abide by the rules which follow:

Know and never underestimate your opponent

As in boxing, football, or any other adversarial pursuit, it is vital to study and to know your opponent; to recognise and to respect strengths and to know and to exploit weaknesses.

The first step, then: identify your opponent. 'Before I agree to come on the programme,' you say to the producer, researcher or reporter, 'who will be interviewing me? If it's John Smith, who stretched me on the rack about this subject last time, I'm not really interested. His questioning was grossly unfair.' That makes it extremely difficult for them to say: 'Yes, I'm afraid it is John Smith.' After all, they want you to appear.

Or you could take a chance by avoiding the leading question and simply ask: 'Who will be doing the interview?' Before you agree to be on the menu, you are fully entitled to identify the chef. If dissatisfied, you can always refuse.

Or ask: 'Am I simply to be interviewed or are your putting someone up against me?'

'It's just you, this time,' comes the reply. Then (once again) you ask who will be doing the interviewing and (this is important) whether your interview will be put into a different context by someone else. Is it perhaps to be used on the endpiece to (on TV) a film, attacking your point of view, or (on radio) a sound clip with the same laudable purpose?

You need to know not only your opponent but the methods. If your contribution is to be related to a film or to someone else's broadcast, you should try to find out in advance what it is. If possible, see or hear it before you broadcast. If they have it on film or on tape, they should let you see it in advance. Second best: watch or listen to it in the studio, before you comment. When asked about it, don't be afraid to reply: 'I did not hear this story until now. It looks like a very one-sided picture, doesn't it? I am surprised that you didn't get comment from the people attacked. I think that we should at least get the evidence on the other side, before we accept any of this apparently slanted material, don't you?' You have started turning the tables, establishing your moderate, central stand – and have avoided the trap that was laid out for you.

Suppose, now, that your opponent (this time, inevitably, the producer), possibly through only receiving the material at the last moment, asks you to comment on a film or tape that comes to you as a complete surprise. Say, bluntly: 'I am shocked that you would ask me to comment on such an important piece without allowing me even to see it. I have always regarded you/your programme as essentially fair – even on subjects upon which we profoundly disagree' (a good and fair line, this one, insufficiently used by victims). 'Recognising that I am to comment without the chance to investigate, all I can say is that the presentation appears at first glance to be a slanted travesty of the truth.'

'Why?' the interviewer must in apparent fairness enquire.

'Because', you say, then launch into your tirade – but make sure that you avoid the perils of defamation (Chapter 70).

As a chosen victim, you may presume that your hosts wish you to perform well, do not want you to dry up, and will want you to feel sufficiently fairly treated to be prepared to return another day. So, willingly or otherwise, they will usually identify your interviewer or your opponent. That gives you time to do some research.

Ask previous victims for a reference. Find out how they induced the interviewer to give them a fair hearing. Consider whether you should warn him or her off in advance ('I know your point of view on this issue – and that it is the same as that of Mr X, whom you are putting up against me. I presume that you will not turn it into a two-to-one battle?').

An interviewer's job is to produce good, lively and probing broadcasts, not to destroy. But watch out for the exceptions to this benevolent rule.

Complaints

It is usually the young and inexperienced interviewer who allows personal passions to intervene with apparent ferocity. The one to watch more carefully is the older, more experienced and cunning bird of broadcast, who destroys by sneer or insinuation, or even by tone of voice. As the old song goes: It ain't what you do, it's the way that you do it . . . It ain't what you say, it's the way that you say it . . .'

Put your complaint about the interviewer into writing; ask loudly enough for a transcript of the broadcast and you will (either directly or via your MP, Senator or Congressman) be sure to get it; and then when the words emerge onto paper, you may find that they appear to be fair – which they were not.

'Is that your real position, then?' can be read in several ways, some of them quite kind. So, next, ask for a tape or video of the broadcast.

Opponents

What, then, of the other sufferers to be thrown into the ring along with you? Again, find out as much as you can about them in advance.

Some opponents will be (in your view) politically wicked but personally kind. My favourite ring partner was Norman Tebbitt, a former airline pilot, who gives as good as he takes, attacks with immoderation and battles to win; who never admits defeat, but who never takes personal offence when he suffers one.

At the end of my interrogation of him before a Parliamentary Select Committee, recorded for later and selective broadcasting, he said:

'Well, that's the sort of constructive approach which I suppose we must expect from a lawyer!' (Thank you, Secretary of State.)

'At least it has more substance than that of a former airline pilot,' I replied, smiling and without great wit, but (as always) the impromptu retort goes down better than it deserves.

One of the joys of our democratic land – and one that is totally inexplicable to those who live in less blessed lands – is that we can so often disagree without being disagreeable. Though even here, clients sometimes get upset when they see their lawyers lunching with their opponents. 'Hypocritical so-and-so,' says the client. 'Criticising and attacking my persecutors in court and then going off arm-in-arm in the interval.'

Good surgeons do not get emotionally involved with their patients, nor good advocates with their clients or cases. One justification for the British legal system, with its remaining distinction between solicitors and barristers, is simply that it keeps counsel at a sensible distance from the lay clients and therefore able to do a better job for them.

So do not presume that your opponents will necessarily be out to do you personal harm. If you see them beforehand, you may even manage to induce them to make useful concessions. Remember Lord Atkin's dictum: 'Cursed is the man who makes a difference of opinion a matter for personal hatred.'

Personal dislike

You may be up against someone who really does equate your case with you, or who has a personal and emotional dislike for both. Then you must look to your weapons.

As always, knowing and preparing your case must have top priority. Unlike the exam student who prepares at reasonable leisure and faces the ordeal, with other victims, in the individual solitude of the silent exam room, you are likely to have little time for preparation and your examination will be very public.

Whatever your dislike for your opponent, try not to show it. The more unpleasant they are to you, the cooler and the more courteous you should become. Aim for viewer reaction: 'That fellow up against you really was a horror wasn't he? If he had had a better case, he wouldn't have had to spend so much time being mean to you?'

Indeed not.

Next, aim at the throat, the gut, the groin. Provided, as usual, that you avoid libel (the category into which broadcast defamation always falls – see Chapter 70), have a go – again with calm courtesy. Follow these guidelines:

Names

Even when your opponents or interviewers are friendly, it is usually better to refer to them by their surnames. First names can sound too chummy, or even patronising. There is an unhappy medium. Instead of referring to 'John' as 'Mr Smith', you can say 'John Smith'. Always remember that even if you are specifically talking to Mr Smith across the table, your real audience is invisible. So address yourself where you can to the interviewer and say: 'John Smith should know better than to say that . . .', instead of: 'You should know better . . .'

Work out in advance what you are going to call the others – and write the names on the paper in front of you, in case stress and memory loss go together.

First and last words

After a particularly bloody radio confrontation, a supporter of mine said: 'You did well – but not really well enough. How could you let that [expletive] get the last word?'

You have no control over who speaks first – the interviewer decides. But you can, in general, commandeer that precious ending.

To cut a speaker off in mid-sentence is far less likely than victims realise. Even during the broadcast, if you speak loud enough, courteously and firmly, those who theoretically control the programme have problems in cutting you off. (They can, however, turn down your microphone, leaving your voice as a background babble.) But if you allow your opponents to keep the ball at their feet most of the time, that is likely to be due to your inexperience, or their skill, or both. The interviewer may (or may not) try to see that you get a fair deal. Grab it – but try to do so gently, courteously and firmly.

The shorter the time, the more important it becomes that you get as much of it as possible for your case. Broadcasting time is both short and expensive. So find out in advance how long your piece is scheduled to last. If it is pre-recorded, then you may be in trouble because any of your words – first, middle or last – may be sliced off. (You may, incidentally, always tell the editor: 'Last time I did this subject for you, you cut off my main point, that . . . If you do it again, that would be most unfair and I shall complain, loudly!')

In any live confrontation – or one which is 'canned' in advance, but unlikely to be cut – you must not only take the last word, but make sure that your opponent does not snatch it back. At best, you simply keep talking until the compere or chairman says: 'I'm sorry, we must close on that note. Thank you John Smith and Jack Jones, for joining us . . .'

At worst, if your opponent is in full flight when the man in charge starts his closing words, you might interject: 'But that really was rubbish, Mr Chairman', or: 'Surely I must be allowed to point out that . . .' then make your point, in a very few brisk words.

'I'm sorry, there's no time for that,' says the interviewer. He loses his 'thank you both', but you have made your point – to the irritation of your opponents and the cheers of your invisible adherents.

Finally, if faced with defeat, there are two basic tactics:

● Announce that you do not accept the decision and that you are fighting back – then do so.

- Flick away the defeat like a fly from your shoulder, pretending that it does not matter. This may be followed by a more subtle fight back.

Praise and condemn

In a confrontation, you must make your opponent's task as difficult as possible. Curiously, that worthy object is often best achieved through damning with faint praise or praising with faint damns. For example: 'I have always regarded Mr Smith's company as one of the highest repute . . . so it is really very difficult to understand how they could now . . .' Or: 'Well Jane Green is an old hand at this game. She has laid her trap with her usual skill – she must forgive me if I do not fall into it. The truth is that . . .' Or: 'Mr White is very influential. Why does he not use that influence to convince his friends that . . .'

Not only does this sort of approach sound good, but it invariably irritates and angers the opposition and, with luck, throws them off course – or, with great luck, gets them really angry.

So how do *you* handle this approach, if used *against* you? Like this: 'I appreciate Mr Black's backhanded compliment – these days, any sort of compliment given to an employer/politician/landlord, etc., is too rare to be rejected. So let's accept that I *am* expert . . . that I do understand the situation/industry/government as well as he says. Then *that* lends weight to my view, which is . . .' Or: 'It is kind of Mr Jones to recognise the high repute of my company. We hold its good name precious. So it is doubly surprising to hear him allege that . . . It is, of course, not a new allegation . . . It is one which our competitors have put about from time to time . . . Still, we take criticism seriously and are fully investigating the matter. If that investigation produces the same results as previous ones – carried out, incidentally, by thoroughly independent consultants, then I am sure that, knowing the high repute of *his* organisation, *he* will immediately, generously and totally withdraw his allegations . . .' You should be so lucky! But you have turned the tables.

Do not be drawn

An alternative ploy to hogging the conversation is prodding the opposition into indiscretion. At its ultimate horror, an interviewer did just that, when he pushed an unfortunate TV panelist called Gilbert Harding into reminiscing himself into tears.

In the unlikely and unhappy event that someone is out for your blood in public and for broadcast destruction, your best rule is – keep silent. Or you may reply, firmly but courteously: 'I am sorry, I'm not prepared to talk about *that*.

You must not of course walk out. Do so and you lose.

John Nott, Defence Secretary, discussing the war in the Falklands, arose in wrath and marched out of TV studio during a TV interview. He received much sympathy from colleagues who had suffered as he did before the cameras. But he hardly enhanced his case. And shortly after, he resigned.

In political life, if you resign you almost always lose – temporarily if not permanently. In broadcasting, you achieve the identical effect by walking out.

You could stay and achieve vast effect by following the Kruschev line. He took off his shoe at the United Nations, and banged it on the table. Harold Macmillan's riposte was classic: 'I wonder,' he said, 'whether we could have that translated into English?'

Far more people are convicted of crimes through opening their mouths too wide than by keeping them closed. Far more civil cases are lost than won through excess speech. In broadcast confrontation, the only time when silence is dangerous is when you are giving the floor to an opponent. Otherwise – and if you are in lone combat with an interviewer – at the first sign that you are drying up, he or she must hand back the baton. Mind how you carry it.

Dodging the dirty question

If you are in court and you deflect a question without answering it, the judge is liable to intervene. 'Please *do* answer the question, Mr Brown,' he says.

Similarly, an interviewer may protest, 'But Mr Brown, you still have not told viewers . . .' Or an experienced opponent may keep hammering – 'I think Mr Brown should answer my question frankly – unless, of course, he would rather not . . .'

You may do the same in reverse: 'Mrs Green has, of course, skirted around my question with her customary skill. But I'd like to ask it again and see whether we cannot get a straight reply . . .'

However, if you wish to avoid answering on a broadcast, you can always succeed – if you know how. A judge may insist on a reply. Neither your interviewer nor your opponents has such power.

So consider in advance the questions that you would least like to answer. Get a colleague or a supporter to interrogate you. Then note down the items to avoid or evade. Your purpose may be legitimate – because, perhaps, to give an acceptable answer would take an unacceptable length of time. Or you may wish to avoid a breach of confidence. Or the reason may be less worthy – perhaps you have overstepped the mark and the point could destroy you, your case or your image, or at least cause it great harm.

So take a leaf out of that book for which politicians are invariably blamed but which is the bible of all skilled presenters and controversialists. Its essence is in the following common quotations:

- 'I'm coming to that point shortly. But first let me finish explaining that . . .'
- 'Now, that *is* an important question. And to answer it, you have to understand . . .' (The ground to which you shift doubtless defies any such understanding.)
- 'I have already answered that question, several times. As Mrs Green well knows, the *real* question – which she quite understandably does not wish to discuss – is . . .' (You may actually be right. Mrs Green may be asking the same question in different words, in the hope of getting a different answer – also a common ploy of the skilled advocate.)
- 'That is the sort of question which is both leading and misleading. The real question is . . .' (Maybe it is . . . but then, maybe . . . Anyway, the ball may pass back and forth several times in court but your Chair or interviewer cannot allow the programme to turn into one of those epic 'Oh yes I did . . .', 'Oh no you didn't . . .' sessions, so well loved by youngsters.

Sit in at Parliamentary Question Time, any weekday afternoon between 2.30 and 3.30. Listen to Ministers *not* answering questions they are asked. Sometimes their opponents get so furious that they yell 'Answer, answer', across the floor of the House. Their fury is often justified but the Minister has the whip hand.

These retorts, resorts and cross-court (or cross studio) returns should be used only when necessary. It is always better to answer a question straight if you can. And if you find that your evasions become skilled, beware of the temptation to use them for fun. Therein lies the path to a perfidious image.

One final example: you talk to children at a local school. No respecters of persons, they may well say to you, 'You tell us that your job is such a good and interesting one. What do you earn?' If you reply, say, £12,000 a year', you will probably be greeted with a whistle of disbelief (not least by children of the unemployed). To them, whatever figure you name is likely to be regarded as exorbitant.

The salary of an MP is a matter of record. But if a local Member is asked to state his pay and he simply replies: 'About £23,000', someone will call out : 'What about the pensioners?', which is in itself a fair question but not entirely relevant.

So *my* answer to *that* question is absolutely true: 'In my case, about enough to pay my expenses. But then I'm lucky, I lecture and write books. My colleagues who have to live on their salaries have a very rough time.' They do. The question has been answered. But a school assembly is no time or place to give the details of financial weight upon a conscientious Parliamentarian.

So answer the question directly if you can; if not, provide an answer that is both true and acceptable; but if you must, be not ashamed to parry the thrust. For example: 'Our annual return shows a gross profit of . . .' Then qualify the answer: 'But we had to transfer an exceptionally heavy amount to . . .'

If silence is the best answer, deflect: 'Compared to other companies in the same business, our profit was acceptable – especially bearing in mind that . . .' To shift attention, always bear everything else in mind.

Interruptions

A good interviewer asks a question and lets the victim get on with answering it. Some interviewers are not so good – and most victims do not answer. So the host butts in.

If you regard the interruption as fair, then stop, but do not be bullied. Say, 'May I finish my sentence, please?', or, 'If you don't mind, I'll just finish this point and then I'll give way . . .' or, 'I'll finish what I'm saying, if I may, then answer your next point.'

In fairness, though, wrap up your point as swiftly as you can. And if the interruption is coming because the programme is ending, finish before you are faded out and never asked back.

Timing

When making a personal presentation – a speech, oration or even a one-person broadcast – you can choose and take your own time.

When engaged in battle, you dare not pause or your opponent or interviewer may simply sit back and let you stew or, more likely, charge into the silence and take over the precious seconds.

If your pause means uncertainty then someone will take advantage of it. If it indicates an area of useful probing, you are in trouble. Get on the road and stay there and do not allow yourself to be side-tracked either by someone else's skill or through your own hesitation.

If you do not know the answer to the question and want time to breathe, ask for it to be repeated – or even take off your spectacles or light your pipe while considering the answer. Or say: 'I can't answer that question.' – dangerous, perhaps, but a touch of modest honesty is sometimes so surprising that it provides an excellent answer. (Unless of course, you should be able to answer and have no excuse for your ignorance, in which case you have lost.) You did not parry when you should have done.

Recognize a friend

If you are asked a difficult question, consider its source. At a political meeting, questions are often asked by some people who really *do* want to know the answer, or so that the speaker will give an answer that can be used by the questioner against mutual opponents, or so that the doubter in the same audience may perhaps be convinced.

Parliamentary questions are rarely asked for information. No one, for instance, is the least interested in knowing from any Prime Minister what are his or her official engagements for the day in question. Mrs Thatcher is asked because *she* is responsible for those engagements and the questioner may then put in an appropriate supplementary question which traditionally begins: 'But will the Prime Minister not take time to consider the plight of . . . ? Or: 'When the Right Honourable lady talks to her Cabinet colleagues today, will she discuss the matter of . . . ?'

By this stratagem, the questioner – fortunate in the daily ballot – can raise any subject that is topical, without reference to the question on the Order Paper which may already have been answered several times. Questioners on the Prime Minister's side of the House usually try to help her. For example: 'Has my Right Honourable friend had time to consider the splendid results of the Government's policy on the control of . . .'

The more sycophantic the question, the more likely that Honourable Members opposite will shout out: 'Give him a job!' No such possibility is open to the Leader of the Opposition . . .

So beware of taking offence when none was intended. The questioner may be on your side. If so, then be grateful. Say, 'That is an excellent question' or, 'Thank you for that helpful and profound question'. Then make sure that you give an equally full and profound answer.

Make your point

You have presumably agreed to go through the ordeal of television or radio, or any other presentation, because you have a case to put, points to make. Then work them out in advance and do not let even the most hostile questioning put you off.

Following the rules on preparation you will have ensured if you can that you are fairly introduced, but if not you will at least slam in from the start with your point of view.

You will have no time to cook your waffle, so stick if you can to one point – or at the most, to two or three. Decide what you want to put over. Jot it down; turn it over in your mind; and if possible toss it back and forth with colleagues.

If you find that the opening and introduction is incorrect or unfair, start by saying: 'I'm surprised that a programme like yours would have put out such a contentious opening. Let me put the other side, right away.' Then do.

If you have followed my earlier advice, you will have prepared yourself. You will know your interviewer and your opponents. You will have checked up on the line of questioning, and if you know your case, you will make your point.

Only beware of over-rehearsal. Parrots never did well at improvisation. Remain alert. Watch out for the unexpected, killer question, and if you get it, battle back. Forget the screen, the viewers, the cameras. Keep your eyes on the opposition – and fight. If you do not win the argument, you will at least win respect.

Jargon

Politicians and lawyers are always and rightly accused of using jargon. To us, it is just as much a form of shorthand as that which you (almost certainly unconsciously) use, for your own business, or commercial or even private purposes.

Business people, doctors, architects, engineers, PR pundits, broadcasters all have their own jargon. But when talking to the unjargonised, avoid it. Use simple, Anglo-Saxon words, brief and vivid analogies, and crisp clear language. Do not believe that you sound more important if you use words that other people cannot understand. They simply get irritated and either take offence or switch off.

Concentrate

If you drive a car and allow your attention to be distracted for a moment, you may be lucky. You may avoid a crash and no one may notice. But you may also hit a truck or (the ultimate in road nightmares) run down a child, or cause some other unnecessary death.

As on the roads, so on radio and especially on TV. You dare not risk a moment's distraction. And while you may be driving for hours on end, your entire TV performance may last only 30 seconds and almost certainly not more than a few minutes. Lose concentration and you lose all.

57 The programme's end

The pilot of an El Al jumbo jet landed his aircraft at New York's
Kennedy Airport. Having finished his usual 'hoping you enjoyed the
journey and that we shall have the pleasure of your company again
soon', he thought that he had switched off. Instead, the passengers
heard the following: 'Marvellous. Now for a cup of coffee and a
woman!' A stewardess rushed up the gangway towards the cabin, to
warn her colleague to close his mouth before an open circuit. An
elderly lady put out her arm and stopped the stewardess in mid-run.
'Take it easy, darling,' she said. 'Give him time to have his coffee!'

As a youngster, I was an addict of BBC Radio's Children's Hour.
The presenter was one Derek McCullough, known to us all merely as
'Uncle Mac'. He was never allowed to forget the day when he became
a victim, to the delight of most, but to the fury of his bosses and of
those who looked after the moral well-being of such theoretically
innocent young persons as myself. His remark was something like
this: 'Well, I guess that will hold the little bastards for another day!'

The pilot and Uncle Mac should have known much better. A
broadcast is never over until someone says, 'Thank you very much.
That's it for today,' or gives some other clear indication that the
viewers or listeners are safely switched away.

'Good night from all of us here at . . .' says the announcer,
mentioning the studio or the programme. 'See you again next week.'
He folds his papers, smiles and nods at the screen – and you believe
that transmission is over. If, however, you have been talking about
famine in Ethiopia, the crash of a business or the effects of a typhoon,
and are now shown loud in laughter, your reputation for sincerity
has gone. *You* know that your laughter is the direct result of release.
The tension is over and you are beaming with satisfaction that at
least you have created no catastrophe. In fact, you have saved your
own until the end.

PART VII

Press, promotions, telephones – and other special techniques

58   The press

The Press – newspapers, national and local – are the oldest of the media. They remain, for reasons of ubiquity and expense, the most commonly used by the business world.

How, then, should you handle newspaper people and make the best of the world of print? Essentially, by doing unto them as you would have them do unto you. With rare exceptions, reporters and editors will react to kindness with generosity, to hostility with patience, to trust with respect, confidence with confidentiality, but to contempt and ridicule with either silence or unfavourable coverage. Call them 'teenage scribblers' (as the Chancellor of the Exchequer, Nigel Lawson, was once unwise enough to do) and they will surely extract their revenge.

Newspapers live by finding and printing news. Churn out for them the old, worn, cliché-ridden press releases and they will be 'spiked', filed, binned, left unused and useless.

Produce a story that is newsy, alive, and aimed at its market and it has at least a reasonable chance of life.

To sell products, you study markets. Apply the same principle to your presentations for the Media. Who are the people whom you really want to reach? Which newspapers are most likely to take which story? Which editor or reporter has a personal interest in a particular theme or idea? Get to know the newspaper people – editors, news editors, features editors, reporters, full-time or free-lance. Ask for their help and you may well get it in unexpected measure.

When I became an MP in 1970, I was warned that the then Deputy Editor of *The Leicester Mercury* was a man to keep at a distance. 'Very dangerous', I was told. In fact, I found him a sound adviser, a wise friend and a considerable ally. The fact that many of his views differ from mine – not least about the politics of his paper – is irrelevant. I respect his professionalism and he mine.

If you have the good fortune to work with press people – local or national – who will be your friends, not only are your presentations more likely to take useful root, but your relations with the Press will be enjoyable, even if you have nothing to report or they find your efforts unworthy of reporting. At least they will 'spike' your press releases, not your goodwill. And if you have a legitimate moan, at least they will listen to it with patience, and do you justice, if they can.

Finally, how do you speak to journalists – perhaps for the first time, on an individual or one-off issue?

Unless you know them well, the rule is, once again: *R*espect and *Sus*pect. Recognise that they will not simply accept spoonfeeding with the story that you want them to put out. Be prepared for cross-examination. Do your homework; prepare your material; know your case – and if necessary, either get help in presenting it yourself or bring in a colleague, skilled in the underestimated art of dealing with journalists.

As in life, so in print – the best is free. Still, you may have to pay – directly, for advertising; or indirectly, for someone to prepare your press release. Even better is to be paid for writing an article which not only advertises your wares, but which can produce reprints, each an invaluable focus for a documentary presentation.

Free print means news value. Editors suffer from chronic shortage of space, but news is the guts of their journals' appeal. From the mighty national to the tiny trade paper, if you provide real news, it will be welcomed. And on the Sam Goldwyn principle that any publicity is good publicity, most editorial comment should be welcomed. Ignorance and silence are the precursors of insolvency.

For news and editorial comment, consider two essentials:

- What news can you make, create, organise?
- How do you best spread the word?

As to making news, watch first class politicians at work. The Media want to headline their efforts on, say, pro-abortion or anti-drug abuse or it-matters-not-what? Then they will find some appropriate Parliamentary or Congressional peg to hang it on – a question, a speech, a motion, a debate.

So, can *you* not open or unveil a new plan, plant or project; an extension, promotion or preview? Or maybe an appointment, reorganisation or massive review of resources? Then try a press conference (Chapter 61) to promote news, real or apparent.

Next, the planted story. Most of the rules are in Chapter 62, on press releases. Your public relations experts should know what to place best – and where, how and through whom. You provide the material at their suggestion.

59   Articles

In an ideal presentational world, you would be paid by others to present your prospective services or products. Ideals are worth working for. The better known you are or become, the more marketable your product, and the more thriving the market place, the more likely it is that editors or producers will invite you to appear on their pages or programmes. Conversely, the less your renown and the worse the recession or depression, the more you will have to go hunting.

To place an article:

- Study and know your market. Which paper, TV or radio programme, or other outlet is likely to use what material and when?
- Find out and approach who actually controls what goes into the paper or outlet. How can you beam in on that individual to best effect?
- Start with a query letter, offering the idea – or kick off with a telephone call, a lunch or a drink.
- Consider whether you can respond to a variation on your suggested theme? Are you able to vary your article or idea to the client's (in this case the newspaper's or magazine's) requirements, as you would your product or your service?
- Consider whether you can meet the likely deadline? Will you need to provide the graphics as well as the text and, if so, will you have the appropriate professional help – journalistic or graphic – available in time?
- If your idea is accepted and your material presented, find out whether it will be changed or sub-edited ('subbed')? Are you prepared for the likely revision?
- Make sure your article stresses the main points in your message – what are they? If you are asked for a biography or bibliography, are they available?

Techniques of article-writing differ only in degree from those used in the best of letterwriting. Remember especially, though:

- To use, but not to overuse, data, graphs and statistics. An article is meant to be read and re-read – often by people with their feet up at the end of a long, hard day. So try to keep down the number of graphs and illustrations.
- To use quotations – sparingly, accurately and, where possible, with attribution.

161

As with letters, so with articles – style counts. Start and end well; structure your sentences and your piece; choose your words with Anglo-Saxon care; avoid the passive, when you can; and do your best to imitate the 'house style' of the journal. Remember: the more your style fits with that of the paper, the less the 'subbing' and the greater your chances not only of publication, but of avoiding the hacking out of those parts which you think the most important, but which the paper may prefer to omit.

So prepare for your market and then organise your mind and your material, before you write. If the material is already on file, perhaps as the basis or in the form of a speech, then knock it into proper form before you ship it out. Few people can give the same words the same impact in both forms.

In speech, you have the advantage of vocal and facial expression to illustrate your words. In articles, both are absent. Conversely, with articles, you can include photographs and graphics. Use them.

In speech, a statement may sound humorous and be accepted as such. In an article, bare of the subtleties of voice inflection, the humour may be replaced by offence, so be careful.

If a book is worth writing, a publisher will normally pay for it. As with books, so with articles. Negotiate your fee in advance, and confirm all details in writing. The fee for a presentational article may, however, be secondary to your need to get the material into printable or reprintable form, so negotiate accordingly.

Finally, check and recheck your article or script before it goes out, for accuracy, grammar and potential defamation.

60 Promoting an event or publicising a promotion

Launching a new product or service, or relaunching an old one? Putting or keeping some aspect of your set-up before the public, local or national? Opening or expanding a branch or a unit? Then how should your presentation be prepared to reach the widest possible public? You will need an event. Harness your ingenuity and that of your colleagues. Where is the best spotlight and how can you focus it on your efforts?

Celebrities earn at least part of their living by 'guest appearances'. Their fees depend on a variety of factors, some of which may conflict. They, too, need a spotlight – but is yours the one for them? Have they a particular interest in promoting your products or services, which will fall in with their need to present themselves in the best light? Will the 'local boy made good' return to his home town, to help put its latest effort onto the commerical map?

In your favour is the sad fact that great names often fall on hard times. Against you, that those on top of the ladder are least likely to turn round and look down – unless, of course, your fee is equally lofty.

Or maybe you can buy your way at an intelligent price into the permanent limelight. It is too late to bathe your products in the glow of Britain's Grand National – Seagrams won that race in 1983 with fine timing. But there are always other worthy causes, willing to give you the benefit of their good name in return for the cash that you would provide for their effort.

Sport, music, theatre – all are looking for 'sponsors'. And if you cannot afford the permanent, then maybe your sponsorship of a local event would attract the oblong eye of the Media?

You could, of course, simply launch your operation or presentation with a press conference see Chapter 61). But for the Press to bother to confer, they will still need an occasion. So at the very least, surely you can find some special event in the life of your company? The announcement of unusual financial news, perhaps? The appointment of a new and notable non-executive director?

Or maybe an anniversary? Birthdays by any name are a fabulous source of notable, unique and historic 'events'. Whose invention marked the start of your line of business? When was the inventor born? What is the anniversary of the launch of the idea?

The anniversary is best if it is a centenary – but a quarter century does nicely. And you can make do with almost any number which ends with a five or a zero or with 13 (bar mitzvah); 'sweet' 16; or 'key-of-the-door' 21.

Even an unpaid celebrity is more likely to come to a 'very special occasion' than to some ordinary gathering. 'We would be deeply honoured,' you write, 'if you would be our guest speaker at a convention to mark the quarter century since the launch of our bank.' Or: 'To mark 25 years since the death of our distinguished founder, we are holding a special exhibition. Would you do us the great honour of opening it, please? Knowing as we do of your interest in . . .' – and away you go.

Combine an occasion with a celebrity and your event is beginning to take shape. Now give plenty of advance warning to the Media. Try sending out a press release, maybe four weeks in advance. 'Cabinet Minister to Open Anniversary Exhibition' runs the headline, or, 'Sporting Hero to Raise Curtain on Birthday Convention.'

A phone call to the advance-planning people at appropriate TV stations or networks with a request that they put your events into their diaries; a word with your friendly editors or newsdesks; a mention in the ear of the radio planners can all be worthwhile. But always build some excitement into the occasion: 'We would not want you to miss it.', 'We are expecting national coverage.', 'We would be surprised if the Minister does not make an important policy statement.', 'Expect fireworks!' Aim to intrigue and entice without giving away too much. For example. 'We appreciate that it is a little way ahead, but we know that you like to note future events in your diary. We think this one would be of special interest to your photographic department. The exhibition is likely to be as spectacular as our guest list.'

Nearer the day, remember to remind. By now, you should have more details. Your presentation will be coming to life, so make sure that your media guests will wish to attend the birth. Say: 'We shall have a special press party afterwards,' or, perhaps: 'The Board would be delighted if you would join us and some other prominent media people for a drink beforehand.'

On the day, the night or the occasion, just hope that the Press will be spared the more attractive joys of wars, massacres, epidemics, bombs and diasasters – especially those near to home. With massive good fortune, they will actually be looking round for news. If you hear them say 'It's one of those quiet days' you're in luck. If, however, you do get deluged in the wake of some great national or international story, so that your presentation appears, if at all, at the foot of page 23 – at least you know you tried. If you do not make an event out of your occasion, you cannot succeed even if the day is otherwise newsless.

According to the classic story, Mrs Brown said to Mrs Green: 'Did you know that Mr White is having an affair?'

'Really,' replied Mrs Green. 'So who's catering?'

If you do not cater for the Media, your affair will go unnoticed.

61   Press conferences

In theory, a press conference is an occasion when the givers confer *with* the Press. In reality, it is an attempt by the givers to confer *upon* the Press the benefit of their latest ideas, activities, products or presentations. In theory, the giver does the Press the courtesy and favour of inviting it to receive important information, without which the newspaper, agency or radio or TV outlet would be bereft; in reality, it is the Media who needs to be seduced into attendance and then fed with stories for which they may spare precious space.

As most executives have about as much idea of how to call and handle a press conference as they have, say, of addressing the Court of Appeal or piloting an aircraft through fog – and as they are far more likely to have to consult with the Press than to endure the other possibilities – here are the basic rules.

No story should mean no conference. Journalists called in to be told of a 'crucial new development for our economy' and then fed some pathetic tale about a revamped product will be far less amused than Queen Victoria. A *con*ference is not an occasion to *con* the Media!

To present yourself, your case or your company to one journalist may be difficult. To do so before a press conference could be much worse. You should carefully consider how and when to call each press conference; where and how to run it – and especially how to ensure that it does not ruin you. To summarise:

- Start with a story. How do you present it so that it reaches your intended audience? If it is limited or local, head for local, regional or specialised media – press, radio or television. If it is major or national and you are creating, building or following-up a story of consequence, then you have two likely courses: you can contact the Press Association or other national news agency, get them to put the story out over their wires, and wait for the Media to come to you. Or: you can set up a press conference – itself an event – and yourself invite the Media to share the story with you.
- Like any other medium or agency, you may contact the news agency through a reporter with whom you have a special relationship. London's top Parliamentary Press Association man is a journalistic genius called Chris Moncrieff. He and his colleagues help MPs to put stories into their own words, which he then sends out. 'Thank you,' he says, 'I'll get that one

moving at once,' which he does, if he thinks that it is worth 'moving' – but which he tactfully forgets if he thinks it is a loser.

When telephoning the agency, or your local equivalent, ask for the news desk (unless you already have a contact there). Like any newspaper, the news agencies and wire services employ people who take down 'copy' by telephone. If you have already thoroughly prepared your piece, you may simply 'phone it through.

Now assume that you decide to call a press conference. Here is a list of the most important rules.

- Choose your time, place and victims with great care – and bring them in by a telephone or written invitation, or by issuing a press release – or both. If dealing with the Press, check by a telephone call to the editor's secretary (a vital ally) that you have asked the most relevant person.
- Make sure the venue is easily accessible. Journalists have a habit of not turning up if they feel that the journey is too far or too difficult, especially if it rains.
- If a newspaper or journal cannot send a representative, make an appointment to visit its office, leaving a sample and your press kit.
- When dealing with a product or service launch (see Chapter 36) do so well before the launch, but put an embargo date on all material (see Chapter 37).
- If people accept your invitation but do not show up, put your press kit and sample in the post or (better) fax it to them that afternoon, so that they can see it as soon as possible. Then ring them to make sure that they have received it and, if possible, arrange a visit.
- When dealing with radio and TV, be sure to choose and contact the correct programmes. Titles are sometimes deceptive, so watch, or listen to, the programmes you intend to contact and note how they present their stories. Keep their requirements in mind when preparing material for them.
- Make contact with the radio or TV programme editor, initially by letter, giving brief details; follow with a telephone call, a few days later. Again remember to act well in advance if you want the item used on the launch day.
- When fixing the time of a press conference, check with three or four of the journalists you regard as most important. Try to ensure that your launch does not clash with anyone else's press conference or reception. Contact your key people first by telephone, to ask if they are able to attend. Ask them to put a pencil note in their diaries, then confirm your telephone conversation by letter and/or by printed invitation, as soon as possible.
- Do not forget that the trade press are usually weekly, fortnightly or monthly publications, and consumer monthly magazines may have as much as a two-month lead-in time between receiving information and

printing it. Always find out which day of the week the trade papers go to press or you may find that on your great day the journalists you most wanted to attend are down at their printers. Once again, if necessary, give details in advance, embargoed.

- If you seek maximum attenance, the best time for your conference is between 10.30 a.m. and noon – before 10, the Media sleepeth, arouseth and prepareth. After noon, you miss lunchtime TV and the afternoon and evening press. Film for evening TV news bulletins and magazine programmes must be processed and 'cut'; likewise, radio tapes must be edited. So morning conferences are usually best.
- You will need to prepare in advance 'press kits', which will be handed out to your press guests as they arrive and sign themselves into the 'Visitors Book' – a necessary record of attendance.
- Radio and TV are often unable or reluctant to use brand names on the air, so make sure that your product is easily identified.

Press kits

A press kit must always look professional. You will need a brochure; a press release – about the product or service and possibly about the company or organisation (see Chapter 62); details of other products or services offered; and prices.

Provide, if you can, a large black and white photograph of the new product with a caption on the back attached securely enough to avoid loss, but not so that the photograph is damaged when it is removed. The photograph should be clear and uncluttered, and printed on glossy paper for best reproduction. (See Chapter 67 on photography.)

Because you will be giving the journalists several pieces of paper as well as the photograph, enclose them in a strong folder, to avoid loss or damage. If you cannot afford specially printed and made up cardboard folders, use clear plastic. If you are providing a product sample, you may need to provide carrier bags. Perhaps your company has stocks of bags already printed with their own logo? Otherwise, plain white plastic carriers will do the job.

Journalists are always happy to have a pre-digest of their media meal. So do provide a handout for each arrival, with carefully prepared, brief and pithy information. The more trouble you save them, *the more likely they are to use your material.*

Content

Do not – ever – invite the Media to receive hard news at your conference and then give one of them the jump on the rest. If you wish, you can mark your press release: 'Embargoed until . . .' That will be honoured.

Journalists are hungrier for news than for sustenance, so there is no need to provide a banquet. If you do, your motives may be regarded as suspect. But a cup of hot coffee and biscuits, or a bottle of beer, or a tot of whisky, shows a touch of humanity and appreciation at any time. Noon and lunchtime conferences require drinks and sandwiches.

While journalists will appreciate sustenance, they will consider themselves misled and their time wasted if the conference does not produce a worthwhile story. After all, a tale worth a paragraph could have been given by telephone. The press conference enables those attending to go into the story in depth; to quiz the participants; to create the 'mileage' upon which their jobs depend.

Now suppose that you have gathered your conference. How do you best handle it and present your case? Do not be inflated or deflated by numbers large or small (respectively). Much depends upon competing news or its absence on that day or hour – over which local politicians, terrorists and other copy-providers have far more influence than your story could ever provide.

Start with the Chair – preferably someone who knows how to deal with pressmen. You have provided each attender with the basis of the story, set out briefly, succinctly and adequately on paper. If you are the Chair, welcome the arrivals; get their names and media origins, both as a courtesy and so that you can identify their likely bias; and after opening the proceedings, hand them over to the presenter of the case.

The presenter should start with something like: 'Good morning and thank you for joining us. Today is the launch of our new product/service'. Or: 'We have called this conference to present to you, as we have done to our shareholders, our annual report and accounts – and to explain our plans and prospects for the future. . . .' Presenters should keep the introduction brief. They will have prepared points in advance; and should present them either as amplification of the press release or in swift succession. Set aside time for questions, but at least give the illusion that you are busy. Your guests certainly will be.

As Chair, call on the questioners, carefully and courteously giving an opportunity to each, but allowing no one to dominate. Accepting the adversarial role of the Press, you will neither try nor still less succeed in protecting anyone against probing or even hostile questions (see Chapter 56). If all know your case and have prepared your defence and counter-attack, that case will survive. If your armour is weak or incomplete, then you will have invited trouble which you could have avoided by simply feeding the information to the Press and not inviting them over your doorstep.

Normally, a press conference need last no longer than about half an hour. Once the formal proceedings are over, individual journalists may wish to ask additional questions privately. Allow them to do so. If radio or TV is represented, the interviewers will want a quiet room or suitable place to operate their magic recording boxes. Make sure that you have one for them.

Whether you are questioned publicly or privately, take care with words. If you need to provide background information or unattributable details, explain your problems to the journalist and your wishes will almost invariably be honoured. In a quarter-century of dealings with the Media, I have never had an unattributable statement attributed to me, or an 'off the record' remark put onto it. Misunderstandings arise through careless communication. If that happens to you, you can probably blame yourself and not the journalists.

Follow-up

Always do a follow-up — a telephone call or a further meeting — with every person to whom you presented your product or service. If you do not chase them up and find out whether the product is going to be mentioned (and if not, then why not), all your efforts may lie forgotten, buried at the back of someone's filing cabinet.

When all is over, hope for the best. Calling the conference is the beginning; getting people to attend and making your presentation is the middle; but the means only justify the end if and when your news actually appears in print, on radio or on TV. You have done your best and so have the journalists. The rest depends on space and on the competition for it. Your skill needs matching with a modicum of good fortune. May you have it, in full measure.

62 Press releases

A press release is a document sent out to the Press or other medium, setting out what its authors would like others to read or hear about the company product, project, or idea concerned. A presentation to the Press should be preceded by a release; and those attending a press conference should certainly receive one. Here, then, are the main rules on the art of releasing your news to the Media.

- Before preparing your release, you must decide: who to send it to; when; and the message you wish to convey.
- Select your recipients with care, otherwise you waste your resources; more important – you misjudge your market.
- Put the release into journalists' language and you vastly enhance its usefulness. Keep it brief, pithy and to the point.
- If all your audiences have the same or similar interests, then one press release will do for the lot. But you cannot always use the same press release for everyone. You may, for example, need to modify or re-arrange the release you send to the trade press in order to make it suitable for consumer publications. They are two different audiences and need separate releases, and possibly even different press conferences. If you combine them at one conference, make sure that the right kits get to the right journals.
- For a professional release, you will need printed paper with the company logo and **News Release** printed at the top of the page. You can use ordinary letterheads, but make sure that you include **News Release** when you print. (See also Chapter 78 on presentations on paper.)
- If ordering paper, check to see what weight of paper your copier can cope with (it is usually about 80 or 90 gms). Otherwise, you may be left with a broken machine and a large pile of scrap paper.
- Date the release – and number it, if applicable. Put an embargo or release date at the top. Put the heading into capitals and *never underline*. To a printer, underlining means 'print in italics', and could cause confusion.
- Always leave a good space between each line (minimum 1½ spacing on a typewriter or word processor) to allow the journalist or sub-editor to alter the release. In that way, your original piece of paper goes right through to the typesetter, eliminating the risk of mistakes creeping in, due to retyping. Leave a wide margin on the left, for printers' instructions.
- Enclose any correspondence or other documents to which the press release refers, and double-check that they *are* enclosed.
- Get the consent of the writer or author of such documents, if necessary.

- If appropriate, include the name, address and/or telephone number of a contact from whom further information can be obtained.
- *Above all*, make sure that you meet deadlines – that press releases arrive in good time to be included in the issue or edition appropriate for your event. The announcement of a future occasion that has already been held is worse than useless!
- If you send out the wording of a speech to be made in the future, be especially careful with the embargo – and ensure that the speaker follows the script, or otherwise carefully informs those media which have already received the release, of any deviation from it. Mark the key passages which you hope will be prominently reproduced.
- When writing the release, headline your message at the start; elaborate it in the middle; and repeat it at the end.
- Recognise that writing a press release requires journalistic expertise. If you do not possess it, yourself or in-house, use a consultant.

63 The telephone – sound without sight

Your smile may be radiant, your personality magnetic, and your appearance may create the perfect image for your purpose, but if your voice is flat, your telephone presentation will land on its back. Yet telephone technique is rarely taught, even to people whose livelihood depends upon it. For the rest, they are expected to cope through trial and error.

This chapter is designed to minimise *your* telephonic trials and errors alike, and to help you to make the best of that inevitably massive percentage of working time which you and your colleagues will spend presenting and persuading by telephone.

Let's start with the voice. As discussed when dealing with radio techniques (Chapter 48), telephone presenters should begin by recording their voices and playing them back. Don't be surprised if you sound like a stranger to yourself – none of us recognises our own voice when we hear it from outside our own head. Then ask yourself these questions:

- Am I conveying charm? It takes no more time to be charming than it does to appear boring or bored, patronising or proud, disinterested or uninteresting.
- Do I sound confident? If you sound timid, hesitant or not in command of yourself, your material, your subject or your intentions, then you can only lose. (It is far easier to feign self-confidence in person, when you can look your prospect, customer or client straight in the eye, than it is by telephone.)
- Do I sound enthusiastic? Whatever you are trying to convey, you should do so with vocal verve and energy.
- Does my voice convey variety – or am I one of those natural telephonic disasters who provide (literally) monotony through monotone? Whatever the undoubted importance of varying your tone, delivery, speed and rhythm when on your feet, change is even more vital by telephone. The longer the call, the more crucial the variation.

Assume, now, that you modestly find some room for improvement in your telephone presentations. How can you best achieve this?

First, use your imagination. Forget that you are communicating by telephone. Seat your listener on the other side of your desk or table – and talk to him or her. Use the converse of TV technique (see Chapter 52), where you normally speak to your interviewer and forget your audience. Imagine yourself in one of those oblique and terrifying studios where you can talk to a screen from which sometimes your own face stares back at you, and conjure up the vision of your victim, instead of allowing yourself to be his or hers. This is not hard when you know the person at the other end of the line. If you have trouble at first in adopting this technique, you could even put the person's photograph before you.

Then forget that you are talking into a machine. Smile and laugh; grimace and gesticulate; even exaggerate your facial and bodily responses; and you will find that these are automatically reflected in your voice. Use the techniques of the long-distance lover, who woos the telephone in his hand, leaving it to the person at the other end to translate vocal feelings into emotion.

Animate the receiver. Have you ever wondered why top-grade television stars, discussion leaders and communicators of all sorts, so often either hold or sit in front of microphones, when modern techniques could leave their hands free? By visibly holding the mike, they instinctively carry a message to their audiences – wooing the mike, and varying volume at their own will, instead of leaving it entirely to engineers or producers.

So use your receiver as a friend; and avoid, where you can, those awful machines that magnify sound. They are useful when, to the knowledge of the other parties, your voice must be conveyed to people other than you. But they provide an inhuman echo – a resonance that banishes the privacy that a telephone can, in theory at least (see later), provide – and they make it doubly hard for you to project your charm, enthusiasm, confidence and persuasion to your listener.

If it is vital for someone to listen in at your end, then get an earphone attached to the receiver. But remember that others do the same. And while you may record a conversation – literally 'for the record' or for whatever purpose – remember that bugs are impersonal objects, available to all.

Some time ago, I negotiated an arrangement with the editor of a local newspaper, to patch up a disagreement which arose entirely through my fault. I was to write a letter on agreed terms, which we hammered out by telephone.

'Fine,' I said. 'So I will write to you and confirm our conversation.'

'No need,' he replied. 'I have it on tape!'

It had not occurred to me that our conversation would be taped without my knowledge. I regarded it then, as I do now, as an invasion of the normal privacy of 'person to person' communication – and ever since, I have treated every telephone conversation as both open and recorded.

This rule, of course, has particular application to overseas telephone calls. If they are not recorded by your overseas communicant, they almost certainly will be by several intelligence agencies. For years, I have talked by telephone to suffering people within the USSR. Sometimes, I have recorded the call, and on occasion, these recordings have been broadcast. The calls are always recorded in the Soviet Union. A journalist who was eventually allowed out to the West told me that when he was interrogated by the KGB, they had played over recordings of telephone conversation which I had had with him. Of course, I had said nothing to him which I did not want the Soviets to hear. But too often, those who speak by phone are careless of the dangers to others.

I once addressed a meeting in an East European country and I asked my host whether he had any advice for me. He replied: 'Say whatever you like. But please remember that if you get a short sentence wrong, I shall get a long one!'

So remember when you speak by telephone, that there may be others listening in – by chance, through a crossed line, or, more likely, by intent. Your words may be recorded, and recorded evidence is generally admissible in court.

Unrecorded calls are ephemeral. Any important conversation should be confirmed, immediately and in writing. When telephoning on any professional or business matter, I keep a dictating machine by my side and, before making the next call, I write, if necessary, to my last listener, perhaps as follows:

Dear Mr Brown,

I was delighted to speak to you by telephone this morning and I most happily confirm my recollection of our agreement. If I do not hear from you to the contrary, I will take it that we may proceed, as discussed. The terms are as follows . . .

Or:

Dear Press Secretary,

Thank you for confirming that I shall be able to speak to your Managing Director on . . . , between . . . and . . . I shall not detain her long – and I am sorry that I was not able to give you details, but the matter is urgent and important.

64 Telephones and time

Telephoning takes time – and time is not only precious in terms of your own minutes and hours, days and weeks – it also costs money. So here is your quick guide to *cost-effective* telephone presentations:

- In theory (but admittedly difficult under business or other pressures) use your telephone when calls are at their cheapest. In broad terms and in the UK, this means: before 8 a.m. and after 6 p.m. on weekdays, or at any time during weekends and statutory holidays. Avoid 9 a.m. to 1 p.m. on working days – or whatever may be the peak hours in the country where you phone.

  Remember that if you are telephoning overseas, the charge is made according to the time and rates in the country where the call *originates*, and on the moment when the call begins – the same rates continue throughout, even if the call runs into either a cheaper or more expensive time after it has begun.
- 'Holding time' is charged at the same rate as speaking time. So if you are asked to 'hold on', whenever possible, decline. Ask to be phoned back; leave your number; and you not only save charges and your own time, but indicate that your time is of importance.
- Preserve your time by getting someone else, where possible, to make your call – and (where necessary) a machine to do the holding on for you. Telephone machinery is sophisticated, computerised, and readily and competitively available. Check sources; compare prices and services; work out which is best and most necessary for you – then buy or rent. If you rent equipment, see if you can beat down the 'minimal rental period' The 'standard terms' are almost always subject to negotiation, but once you have signed up, you will probably have to pay for most of the full period, even if (through removal or any other cause) you want to cancel.
- Whether you instruct a telephonist, secretary, or assistant to take your calls, train him or her to act as a conduit and a buffer. If you are making the call, he or she will be responsible for getting you through to the right person, and not readily taking no for an answer. If you are waiting to speak, he or she should not say: 'This is John Smith's office' but 'I have Mr John Smith to speak to your Managing Director. The matter is urgent. Can you please put me through?'
- If the person you are telephoning is actually or allegedly busy, out or away, do not give up. Emphasise the importance and urgency of the call, and if you still cannot get through to the person you want, ask: 'Would it be convenient to call back in half an hour/this afternoon/tomorrow

morning?' Say: 'Will he be phoning in? If so, please would you ask him to telephone me/Mr Brown at . . .' – then give him the numbers.

- Get the name of the person taking the message, and ask to speak to him or her next time. This personalises your approach (even more important by telephone than when the person is before you), and increases the sense of urgency by repeating the message to the same person.
- When you eventually speak to the right person work from notes or a checklist. This will not only help you to cover your points quickly, but will ensure that you do not have to go through the same hassle and waste of time and money is calling again because you have forgotten something important.
- Then note – either personally or via your secretary or assistant – the guts of the call, including any agreement reached; any important statements or admissions; and any follow-up action required.

If you are brisk and businesslike and show that your own telephone time counts, you will not only save time (and the money it represents), but you will convey a businesslike impression that will help achieve the results you want, through your telephone presentation. You will keep up appearances, keep down the bills, and use the telephone to its best advantage.

Another reason for keeping telephone calls short is to avoid saying too much. Conversely, if you are trying to get someone else to 'open up', listen attentively. At any time, it is easier to be a good talker than a good listener. At no time is listening more crucial than by telephone.

Suppose, for instance, that you are dealing with an experienced journalist who is trying to 'pump' you for information. You have decided what you want to say and, if you are wise, you will have jotted it down. He or she will be trying to relax you; you will try to send him or her away satisfied, but with as little information as you wish to give.

The battle is on. Journalists are expert at using telephones. Most get the majority of their material that way. And as most people talk more by telephone than in person, the journalist will try to keep you chatting away until he gets what he wants.

Your response? Once again: conjure up the image of the interviewer; pretend that he or she is carrying on the confrontation face to face and with your colleagues listening; and avoid saying anything by telephone that you would not say in public, in person, or at a press conference.

There is only one exception to this good rule. Journalists worth their professional salt will honour 'off the record' information. Provided that you make it absolutely clear that the information you give *is* 'off the record', the chances of its improper use are small.

The conversation goes something like this: a journalist asks, 'What happens next?', or, 'Why did you say this?', or, 'What are you going to do about such-and-such?' You are not prepared to say much 'on the record' – for her to quote as she sees fit. But you do want her to know the full facts.

You have nothing to hide and you want her co-operation, so you can continue. For example: 'On the record, Jean, the situation is . . . Now, may I please tell you something more, 'off the record'? The journalist may in theory say: 'No, thank you. I do not want to know anything that I cannot quote.' But she will normally reply: 'Go ahead.' You can then tell her why the information about to be given must be 'off the record' – either permanently or for the moment. For instance: 'You will appreciate when I tell you, there is some very personal information here.' Or: 'If we go public on this before . . . then it can do a great deal of harm.' Or: 'It will kill off the story if we let it be known in advance.' Or: 'The security boys have specially asked us to say nothing about this aspect of the matter.'

The journalist may, quite properly, listen to the 'off the record' material and then urge you to allow her to publish all or part of it. If you do not agree, she should honour her word.

Warning: always, ALWAYS make it sufficiently clear to the journalist that the information you are about to give is 'off the record'. Of course the only way to keep anything really secret is to keep it to yourself – and (once again) if you are speaking by telephone, there can be no guarantee that somone else is not (deliberately or through an accidental crossed-line) listening in.

Still, while journalists may want you for your story today, you may need them for your purposes tomorrow. Trust and information given are generally returned.

Finally: do train your staff in telephone techniques. If you have to learn them yourself, then don't assume that anyone else, presumably less experienced and skilled than you, will know them. A little telephone training goes a long way, while its absence is as notable as it is costly.

A warm, efficient, properly prepared, natural and, where necessary, well rehearsed conversation style – pleasant, authoritative and timely – is crucial to successful telephone presentations. And where, for any reason, it is either impracticable or too expensive, then write. The telephone is an alternative to the word processor or to the pen, not a substitute for either.

65   Photographs

The camera does indeed lie. But in truth or in falsehood, it provides a most valuable presentational weapon, if you know how to use it.

You should employ photographers to create (literally) your image, or that of your company or organisation. Employed full-time as your own 'tame' operatives, you will be able to train them into your needs and requirements. More likely, however, you will bring them in – freelance and for the occasion. So how do you get the best from them?

First, explain your requirements, with as much precision as possible. Do you, for instance, want a 'mug shot' six by four inches on glossy paper, for sending out with a press release? If so, then do you prefer to be shown as happy, smiling, radiant and confident – or as thoughtful, serious and profoundly intelligent? Or should you not have both types in your file – 'the smiler' is no more likely to be appropriate for a piece explaining the recent decline in your company's profits than 'the misery' for the opening of your new branch or factory.

Or do you need an action shot, showing you, perhaps, inspecting the works, addressing your sales force, or chairing a meeting? The photographer will decide whether or not to organise a pose or to act as fly on the wall, but only after you explain your wishes.

Second, if you have picked the right people to do the job, then let them get on with it. Accept instructions on where and how you sit or stand, talk or move, twist your body or your head. If you are dissatisfied with their work, then they will lose a client, so put your trust in their wish to please you. You will probably pay a basic fee for attendance and expenses, but their real profits will only come if they sell you their work in bulk.

Third, work out your terms in advance. At best, buy the copyright, so that you can reproduce the photographs you like, as, when and where you see fit. Otherwise, negotiate in advance for the rights you will require at a fee you are prepared to pay.

Photographers operate on the open market and sell at whatever prices they can negotiate. In general, you get what you pay for, so if you want top experience, you must expect to pay top prices.

You will receive 'contact' sheets of rough prints for proofs. You can either leave it to the photographers to enlarge those that they think are best, for your instant approval (a desirable system if speed is important), or you can mark your preferences on the sheets.

The fun begins when you receive the enlargements. The photographer, or some other expert, can touch up the original with magical skill. Your beauty can become rampant and your blemishes disappear, warts and all. Whatever miracles may be performed on your person may also be done for your premises, the landscape, or anything else on print. Lenses, lighting and adroit photography make the camera lie. But the real deception begins with the refinished photographs. Touched up photographs are the ad-man's stock-in-trade – and they are available for purchase, by you or your business.

Where an event is photographed, time is the essence of success and the photographer's skill must be immediate. If you are presenting a new product, then make it an occasion. Invite the press, local or national – but speak specifically to the photodesk. Tell them why the event will make a good picture story, and ask them to send their photographers. Then create a picture worthy of their time.

You could start with the traditional group, perhaps clustered around the product with you pointing joyfully at your brainchild. Or maybe the most handsome person in your employ could substitute for the chairman's wife smashing a bottle of champagne on its bows.

Or, as names are news, consider whether it would be worth your commercial while to bring in some celebrity, to be photographed together with you and the product. Or perhaps you could induce the appropriate Minister of the Crown to do so as a service to your industry? Then name the celebrity in the caption – otherwise too many readers will only recognise a familiar face.

Celebrities' fees are negotiable. Ministers and MPs are strictly limited in the gifts which they are entitled to receive. If you want to give the Minister a present, however modest, check first with his or her personal assistant. Presentations of this sort must be open and manifestly proper.

Whether you present your image solo, or in company with important people, preparation pays. Failure to prepare for your photographer means that you may have to pay for useless results. So next time you are asked to say 'cheese', consider whether some other sound might not be more appropriate, to project the correct photographic image for the actual or intended occasion.

To see how others get their photographic presentations into print, pick up the business section of any Sunday newspaper. There are the three directors of a bathroom fittings company sitting in swimming trunks in one of their own products. There is the director of a toy factory, being hugged by a massive Mickey Mouse. Everywhere there are smiling people, presenting their wares.

When the camera makes a story, rather than recording it, the Press takes an interest. Both the 'quality' papers and the tabloids have practically the same single interest – to ensure that they keep their readers. A bright and unusual photograph banishes boredom – a dull one lands in the bin.

PS: If you want to be on other people's photographs, arrive early. Photographers have deadlines, beds, wives and husbands. They usually turn up at the beginning of a meeting, concert, or function, take their photographs as swiftly as they can, and then get out. If the purpose of your visit is to get your photograph – or that of your product or service – into the Press, then get there well before the start.

66   On the move

Mobile presentations range from the simplicity of a loudspeaker to the sophistication of portable exhibitions – from skywriting by aircraft to advertising by balloon.

Mobile loudspeakering is an election essential and an advertising occasional. If you wish to use a speaker to advertise an event, check on local bye-laws. You may find, for instance, that all is legal provided that (as in the City of Leicester) you keep your appropriate distance from, for example, the clocktower.

The more powerful the loudspeaker, the greater its likely effect. Hand-operated machines are fine if you are talking from the roof or back of your vehicle to a throng of listeners, but they are generally useless on the move.

Use the best equipment and you can whisper into the loudspeaker and boom your message, literally, through the walls of houses. The techniques are simple but vital:

- Keep your message extremely brief – no more than half a dozen pithy phrases. By the time you have attracted your listeners' attention and spoken your words, your vehicle will have passed on. Use two loudspeakers, one facing forward and one to the rear, and you double your prospects of your message striking home.
- Stop your vehicle at the end of a street. 'Good morning Kensington Street, good morning Kensington Street. This is Robert Edwards, your exhibition organiser. Good morning Kensington Street, good morning Kensington Street. This is Robert Edwards, your exhibition organiser. Today's the day . . . Hog's Hotel is the place . . . 12 noon is the time – come to Hog's Hotel at 12 noon . . .' Then start moving forward, slowly. By then, people will have had time to tune in with their ears, and to come to their doors. Curiosity is a mighty magnet that takes time to work. Once moving the message should be even shorter – '12 noon . . . at Hog's Hotel . . . show today . . . 12 noon . . . Hog's Hotel . . . at 12 noon . . .'
- Pronounce each word separately and clearly: 'Good – morning – Kensington – Street. Hold the microphone close to your mouth – and adjust the sound level on your loudspeaker so as to achieve maximum volume without risking the almighty screech. If you are operating in a canyon of housing, the volume must be reduced. If you are disturbing the peace of the open countryside, then the volume may be safely raised.
- Keep your batteries charged – and your equipment guarded. Allow either

184

your vehicle or the equipment to become inoperative and your message goes silent.

- Finally, get an experienced driver to steer the vehicle out of trouble, leaving you to concentrate on the loudspeaker. The lower your speed, the more you are likely to upset other vehicles. The greater the attractions of your loudspeaker, the more the children who are likely to run out from between parked vehicles and under your wheels.

It is irresponsible and potentially dangerous to drive while under the influence of a loudspeaker. Divide your functions – the driver drives and the operator speaks.

To keep speaking while controlling the driver, agree hand signals – a sweep of the wrist, perhaps, to move forward; an up-and-down motion to go slow; an open hand to stop. Agree whatever you like and then stick to it – but the driver must clearly understand that whatever signals he or she receives, *safety has top priority and overrides all instructions.*

Imagine the headline: 'Bloggs & Co. Exhibition organiser runs down child. "I was concentrating on my loudspeaker," said Mr Bloggs.' The ultimate nightmare.

67 Groups

All MPs spend a fulfilling and frequent part of their lives as tour
guides, escorting constituency schoolchildren, overseas colleagues,
friends and family, and that most irritating and time-consuming
category of all – the alleged friends of friends or family. For example:
'Your Aunt Martha specially asked me to telephone when we were
passing through London,' says the voice, 'and to give you her
love . . .'

'And, I suppose, to say that you would like to look round the
House?'

'Well, how *did* you guess?'

So we all learn to make presentations to visitors. Your equivalent
may be the top-level guided tour of office, works, factory, or even of
the United Kingdom or parts of it, for actual or potential customers
or clients – or simply showing friends or family around your locality.

For you and for me, I have searched in vain for a quick guide to
swift, satisfactory and sensible mobile or touring presentations. So
that is where we begin. We end with some suggestions on how to
cope with similar operations, inflicted on you, or on parties that you
lead, by other presenters.

Before you start your perambulation, you must consider:
(a) object; (b) importance; (c) timing; and (d) delegation.

If the purpose is to please important clients, then timing depends
upon their convenience, not yours; and you can only delegate those
aspects which you are prepared to admit that someone else knows at
least as well as you do. If time management requires you for some
more important effort, and if the object of the presentation is less
crucial or more easily accomplished by others, then the tour can be
shortened and you can delegate much of the presentation to others –
perhaps all of it other than either a welcome or a farewell from you.

If you are responsible for accompanying or addressing the party, it
helps to know what you are talking about – but this is not always
essential. While it is unwise to make up stories for visiting historians,
an introductory: 'Now, this is a well-known tale about Westminster
Hall. I cannot vouch for its accuracy, but . . .', may let you off the
hook.

In most cases, though, you simply tell your guests about how

Charles II dug up the body of Oliver Cromwell, cut off his head and put it on a spike projecting from the roof of that Great Hall, where it remained for some seven years (all true), followed by the (infinitely jollier) story of how it dripped blood steadily onto the flagstones. 'If you look carefully, you will see the remains of Oliver Cromwell's blood,' you say, pointing at some splodges of black tar.

'Horrible!' chorus your audience – and probably remember that story more than anything else you tell them – and certainly far more than the number of rooms in the building, or miles in the corridors, or steps in Big Ben, or which architect built what in which century, and what was burned down and why, and who decided to save Westminster Hall rather than the Chamber of the House when two incendiaries fell on the place during the last war, or any of the other items of useless information which stream breathlessly, and without pause or verbal punctuation, from the guides and their Parliamentary disciples, to the never-ending stream of tourists who pass through the Palace of Westminster each day.

Transfer this routine to your own circumstances and the lesson is obvious. Unless you are dealing with people who have a professional or commercial interest in detail, skip it. To you it may hold the ultimate fascination, but to them it is statistical death warmed up. Forget, if you can, what interests you and consider what is of concern to them.

Most presentational pomposity is bred by thoughtless conceit. You think that because some subject fascinates you, then it must at least interest others? Rubbish. Your passion for computer technology, architectural eccentricity or the sex life of a glow worm may, and no doubt will, appear to you totally normal. To others, it is as absorbing as you would no doubt find my love of ancient Roman glass or the involvement of workers in industrial decision-making in a Peruvian factory or an Israeli kibbutz.

Long speeches to standing victims are a menace. Apart from those who (like myself) suffer from backache, which turns standing minutes into agonising hours, even the totally fit resent long wind at their standing expense. If they can drift away, they will. 'I am so sorry, but I forgot that I have to be back in my office in ten minutes', 'Good gracious, it's half past three. I am so sorry to interrupt you, but I must get away.' Epitaphs, these, on too many presentational tombstones.

Assess visitors' interests alongside their importance and put your time and that of your colleagues, staff or family into the balance, and you should emerge with a product that will be appreciated. Now you are ready to put it on the market.

Talks or speeches are pointless unless they are heard. Watch out for acoustics when you are on the move. Yelling above the noise of machinery is bad for lungs and eardrums alike, so explain in advance; take questions in arrear; and use gestures to penetrate noise. Remember, too, that if safety equipment – including ear protection – is properly worn by people working in the area, it should also be supplied and worn by visitors, and especially by you.

If you are taking your guests on a tour bus, make sure that it has an operative microphone at the front. The driver should switch it on for you, or, if you have professional guides, then do not be too shy to take it from them. Then experiment with the temperamental object to see whether it works best when held in front of your mouth or below your lower lip, or when held horizontally or vertically. If the coach is moving, try to keep the microphone away from your teeth or you may lose them and your words at the first monster jolt.

Ask people at the back, 'Can you hear me clearly?', and, unless you get a unanimous chorus of affirmation, try again. Mobile amplification is sometimes even more unwilling to co-operate than its land-based equivalent. When you and the equipment are both shaking, your prospects of synthesised vibration are not great. It may be better to stop the bus, fill your lungs and ditch the amplification.

If your voice is weak and the distance it must travel is great, do not despise those shoulder-carried amplification systems which are the transistorised baby brothers of the more common and larger versions. As with a radio, so with a loudspeaker – to some extent, size determines effective volume.

Finally: some words on mobile leadership, so often needed as an adjunct to mobile presentations.

First, go with, eat with and (where appropriate) stay with, your party.

I once met a Swede who was completing twelve months' study of British management. I asked if she could encapsulate in a few words what she thought was worst in that management. She replied without hesitation: 'Most of your businesses operate a class system. Directors, top managers, middle managers and the staff eat separately, have separate toilets, and in some places even use different-quality toilet paper!' Do not apply this principle to your guests – by, for instance, putting them into a rickety bus while you travel in your executive limousine, or letting them stay at your local inn while you relax five star. The worse *their* circumstances, the more they will resent *yours*.

Do you remember Gilbert and Sullivan's Duke of Plaza Toro, who led his army from the rear? The best leadership is from the front, 'After me . . .' It is said that a certain nation used to require its womenfolk to walk a couple of paces behind their men, until the discovery of landmines, since when they have walked a couple of paces in front. Effective group leaders must take their chance with landmines.

Second, as always, listen before, during and after you talk. Before, so that you know what your victims wish to hear; during, so that you sense whether or not your presentation is producing its effect; and after, so as to answer questions and discover whether you have covered the necessary ground.

A Foreign Minister was incredibly unpopular with his senior staff. 'It's not that we necessarily want him to do what we suggest,' one of them told me, 'although of course that would do neither him nor the nation any harm! It's simply that he doesn't bother to listen before he makes up his mind. So what's the point of employing us?' A colleague added: 'It's not that he has enemies. It's that his friends can't stand him!' The best leaders listen — and then make their decisions, take responsibility for them and stick to them.

Third, keep the group together. Avoid drift, and explain how and why. Take individual idiosyncracy into account, but tell people why they cannot expect to flake off, and why they must accept a degree of discipline, subject only to the calls of nature.

As leader, you will be expected to express the views or feelings of the group to the others — whether words of complaint or thanks, of greeting or farewell, explanation or exhortation. But you must also handle them with all the charm, guile and tact which will make your listeners believe that they are acting of their own volition, which you do no more than interpret.

68   The great outdoors

Outdoor presentations require specialised planning, equipment and techniques. Gripping and holding an audience out of doors is almost always more challenging than inside. Move acoustics outside a room, hall or building and they may become both different and worse.

The amplification equipment used by the Pope to enthrall his flock in St. Peter's Square is magnificent. You hear the Pontiff's words as if they were whispered into your ear, even if you see him only as a distant, white speck on a grey balcony.

So, if you are speaking out of doors to any more than a handful of folk, make sure of your equipment. If it fails, so will you. Take care, too, that it is well sited. Your venue may leave you with no choice of platform, but you must still select, site, and regulate your equipment – and get expert assistance.

Orate from the plinth at Trafalgar Square and your words must be spoken slowly – each will rebound from the marbled walls of the National Gallery. But most venues give scope for choice, though loudspeakers are sometimes forbidden. The orators of Speakers' Corner at Hyde Park must entice and hold their audiences through the bellows of their lungs. But the police and park authorities will allow loudspeakers for meetings in the parkland behind it.

Once you know that your audience will hear your words, you must then choose them to match the place and the occasion. If your hearers are standing, take pity upon them and be brief. If they are seated, then you may pronounce, slowly, longer sentences on them, without fear of complaint. Avoid jokes in the open air – they die.

Unfortunately, outdoor atmosphere is hard to create, unless you have a packed and excited meeting, tense and expectant. Address 2,000 people in the Albert Hall and the place is an echoing morgue. Pack a quarter of that number into the hall of your local church and your words will take off. If you have a choice between a place where all your audience will sit comfortably but some places will be empty, as opposed to a hall where some may have to stand around the sides, opt unhesitatingly for the latter. Latecomers will be sorry and next time will arrive earlier, and your presentations will have the benefit of that electricity created by a crowd.

Now transfer the same operation out of doors. How do you fill the surface of the earth? Yours is not the miracle of Cecil B. de Mille, with his thousands of rent-a-crowd extras. You cannot gather your disciples at your feet to pronounce some modern sermon on your local mountainside. You will bring your audience as closely together as you reasonably can and as they are prepared to accept – and you will then compete with the birds and the bees, in their less exotic moments; with aircraft roaring and droning overhead; with traffic on the roads, dogs on the paths, horns on the move, etc, etc.

Consider your course of action if it then rains, hails, or snows. Must your presentation be destroyed or could you prepare a haven in a marquee or hall for such contingencies? You could, of course, take out what insurers call a 'pluvius' policy – you buy compensation, linked to some specified rainfall. But your presentation will still have been washed away.

So before you prepare a presentation for out of doors, consider whether you could not produce a much better operation inside. If not, then at least have a plan to move indoors if the weather comes to its unpredictable worst. And if the open skies are for you, then remember that the effect of your message is likely to be in inverse ratio to its length. Out of doors, the shorter is definitely the better – and the unheard is the failure.

69 Elections

Elections mean that politicians must present themselves and their parties in the best possible light. Democracy is fine if you win, but there are no consolation prizes.

Election presentation spreads throughout all our institutional life that is not fundamentally feudal – which means, to many posts inside and outside the world of commerce and industry. Academics at universities; churchmen at convocations; members of societies at their Annual General Meetings – all must, at some time in their lives, present themselves for election to one office or another.

In party politics, individuals count less. But the personal vote is greatly underestimated. A mercurial colleague stood in a Leicester by-election when the incumbent had become a High Court Judge. He was asked by the local newspaper whether he expected to be elected. 'Of course,' he replied, 'A horse with Labour colours would win here!' The following day, a caricature appeared on the front page of the newspaper, showing the candidate riding a scrawny horse, with Labour colours behind its ear. The candidate protested that he had been gravely misunderstood but the newspaper and its reporter were unrepentant. He lost the election, but was later elected as Labour MP – before deserting to the SDP, whereupon he promptly lost his seat. Horses for courses . . .

So Rule Number One must be: beware of over-confidence. If you are coming up for selection as a candidate, take heed of Austen Mitchell's warning (in his excellent book, *Westminster Man*) against being ahead too early. All other contestants will then gang up against you and push you to the rear. Still, if you are a horse who does better when out in front, you should at least convince yourself that you are in the lead.

Second, however confident you may be, do not burn existing bridges. Recognise the vagaries of any electorate and the certainty that elections are only won or lost when the ballot papers are actually in the box. Until then, anything can happen – and frequently does. This adds spice for the public; a perverted delight when the pollsters make their inevitable errors; and misery for the victims, whose life's work may depend upon the result.

Nor are the criteria upon which elections are won and lost always what you might expect. It is generally believed that if your name is high up in the alphabetical order of candidates, you will acquire a number of votes from people who work down a list rather than vote for a particular candidate. So if your name is Brown, maybe you should change it by deed poll to Aarons or Abse?

To win an election, you should seek the maximum number of authorised voters – and make sure that your side turns out at the poll. Prepare a checklist, thus:

- Who are the potential voters? Do they have to register and, if so, with whom and by what date? Can you achieve a greater registration of voters who are likely (or even better, certain) to go your way?
- In company elections, can you accumulate proxies? In political ballots, have you worked sufficiently on the postal vote? In selection conferences, have those wards or organisation within your party that are most likely to vote for you registered their maximum potential? (My son was beaten by his woman opponent in the battle to become General Election candidate for a marginal seat, after she had registered, at the last moment, three women's branches. Each branch had two delegates to add to the rural branches already registered.)
- Are the potential voters duly qualified? Do they, for instance, have the appropriate shares? Have they been members of the party or organisation for the period required by the constitution? (Check this one with special care. In the Labour Party, for instance, any member may take part in a ward meeting which decides whom to support as its candidate for a General Election, but in order to be a voting member of the General Management Committee which carries out the actual selection, the person must have been a member for at least a year and normally have attended at least one meeting during the course of that year.)
- Conversely, are you able to challenge any of your opponent's would-be electors?
- Organise, encourage, promote and solidify your supporters, and disregard the rest. Whether you are dealing with the government of a country or of any organisation within it, you should recognise that you can afford to ignore or even to antagonise those who will not vote for you anyway. But if you fall out with your own supporters, you are lost. So rally your own troops; spend your resources – physical and financial, in time and in energy – to bring in your own forces behind you. If you are able to deflect some of your opponents' support in your direction, then (as the Australians would say) 'Good on you'. But it is your own backers who will put you in front.
- Have you prepared your campaign so as to produce the personal and/or group image that will best please your supporters? Start with your party programme. A political platform should not be like a platform of a bus –

something merely to get in on and not to stand on. You must convince your electorate (political, commerical or otherwise) that your cause is genuine, sincere, and for their benefit.

- Personal image is greatly underestimated. A family man or woman leading a reasonable, decent sort of existence; the person who cares for the concerns of his or her electorate; the candidate with the good name – he or she will attract a personal following and the votes of even some who disagree on policies or platforms.

- How much money can you spend – recognising your resources and any limits on your legal right to spend them? How do you best use the money you have? Do you, for instance, put out any (and if so what sort) election address or pamphlet? Do you send out circulars – and if so, do these go by post? In political elections, how much do you spend on window bills, car stickers or posters – and what size or what shape best fit windows in your area (has it occurred to you that window panes vary hugely – from estate to estate and sometimes from house to house)? In the USA, what can and should you spend on television adverts or appearances?

- When preparing an advertising presentation, do you consider the best media for your purpose? You must do the same for every type of presentation that is intended to lead to your selection, election, re-selection or re-election.

- Finally, have you done all in your power to ensure that your voters get to the poll? If they are elderly or infirm or both, do they need transport and if so, will cars be available? If not (here we go again) do the rules permit postal or proxy voting, and if so, have you helped to make the necessary arrangements? Do your voters remember the date and the time of the voting and have you done what you should to remind them?

Election presentation is part of the overall organisational process that decides on the government – of a democratic country, however, large, or of a company, corporation or other organisation, however large or small. It is an art, a skill, a discipline. It requires dedication, experience and much good luck. If the tide flows strongly enough in your direction, it will sweep you in – while if the landslide cascades against you, no campaign will put you on your electoral feet. But in a tight corner, the right presentation may easily make the difference between victory and defeat. Get in by one vote and you can win and laugh. Defeat by the same minimal, miserable margin means electoral disaster.

If you stand for office, I wish you luck. And if you must lose, then I hope that it will be by a margin large enough not to leave you worrying about which items on the checklist you forgot to follow.

70   Libel and slander

The greatest legal danger to the presenter is: defamation. Where you speak ill of others, you must watch your words or risk retaliation. So here is the presenter's guide to this complex and unhappy area of the law.

Definitions

A statement is 'defamatory' if it would 'lower' the person referred to 'in the eyes of right-thinking people'. So if you call someone a cheat, a liar or a rogue; if you allege that he is bad at his business; or corrupt or negligent in his dealings – then you 'defame' him.

A defamatory statement made in writing or in any other permanent form – including television or radio broadcasting – is a 'libel'. The same statement made orally is a 'slander'.

Libel is easier to prove, because the evidence is on paper or on tape and (broadly) it gives the victim greater rights in more varied circumstances. If slander can be proved it is usually equally 'actionable'.

'Justification'

No one is entitled to an unearned good name. So if the defamatory statement is substantially correct, then it is 'justified' and the victim will get no damages.

If defendants plead 'justification' and fail, then they have repeated the defamation – loudly and publicly – and the damages will multiply.

'Fair comment'

The law generally protects people's rights to express opinions – as opposed to mis-stating facts. So you may comment on a matter of public interest, even if that comment is unfavourable to another individual or company. Even if the comment is not 'fair' ie, in the sense that it goes beyond good sense and decency, it will not remove the defence.'Mere vulgar abuse' will not give its victims any legal rights.

'Privilege'

The law recognises that freedom of speech must sometimes be absolute. So no defamation action can ever be brought against MPs for what they say in Parliament. But outside Parliament, an MP has no more protection against defamation actions than anyone else – although the temptation to provide the material for them is never-ending. So great is the risk that no insurer will provide cover for an MP against defamation actions arising from political duties.

So if your conduct is impugned by an MP in the House, you could issue the traditional challenge to repeat the statement outside Parliament. But do not be surprised if the Member simply smiles and continues to campaign, under the shelter of absolute Parliamentary privilege.

The same complete cover applies to statements made by any person in any capacity in any court. The downfall of former Liberal leader Jeremy Thorpe began with a devastating outburst in entirely irrelevant court proceedings.

'Qualified privilege'

In some circumstances, the privilege to defame may be 'qualified'. *NB*: the law recognises that no business person is bound to provide either a trade or a personal reference, yet the giving of references is commercially necessary. Providers of references give information under a moral duty to others who have a direct interest. So the occasion is 'privileged', but subject to one qualification: if a defamatory statement is made out of 'malice', then the privilege is destroyed.

'Malice' for this purpose means any unlawful motive – in general, the wish to harm the person defamed, rather than the wish to assist the recipient.

However, defamation cases arising out of references are almost unknown. Legal aid is not available for defamation actions, and contents of references are difficult to prove. Statements made are likely to be 'justified', ie substantially true. And anyway, the occasion is subject to 'qualified privilege' – and 'malice' (in the legal sense) is difficult to prove.

In practice, the greatest legal danger in the giving of references comes not from defamation but from negligent actions, ie, from an incorrect reference, personal or trade, given carelessly. You may avoid the peril of negligence actions by adding the magic words 'without legal responsibility' to all references. (Pleasanter wording: 'While we are pleased to provide trade/personal references, we do so without legal responsibility'.)

Avoiding trouble

The only positive way to avoid risk of defamation is to emulate the monkey who held his hands over his mouth and said nothing. Speak ill of others only if you are prepared to defend yourself against retaliation. Present your own case with maximum praise – but take care how you represent the evils of your adversaries.

PART VIII

Endpieces and checklists

71   Endpiece

Presentation is personal chemistry. Study and follow the rules and adapt them to your own style and talent and you increase your chances of success. But you cannot win them all. So do not despair when you lose.

If this book has helped you to maximise your prospects of success and to minimise your failures, it will have served you well. The fact that you may have bought or borrowed it in the wake of disasters should help you to avoid others.

If your failures are occasional, you will be forgiven by others, if not by yourself. If you study and follow these presentational skills and success continues to elude you, then you will be thrust back on that sad old truth: 'Nothing succeeds like a successor!' You will pass the buck to someone else, whom you will select as a potential presenter, and will devote yourself to making your mark and your millions in some other way.

Remember the story of the man who applied for a job as a clerk but was turned down because he suffered from dyslexia? So he rented a clothing stall in a market and ten years later had built up a mighty business. Interviewed by *Time Magazine* and asked to what he attributed his success, he replied: 'To my failure! Just think where I would not have been today, had I only got that job as a clerk in your office!'

To pull the threads together, here is a checklist of some of those plans for *action* that you may wish to make, having absorbed, approved and accepted the propositions in this book.

- List the presentations that will need to be made by or on behalf of your company, firm or organisation within the next few months.
- Consider in respect of each such presentation, by whom it should be made – whether by an individual or a team and, in either case, who would do the job best?
- Arrange appropriate training *now* for each person who will need it in due course. Remember: training must be followed by practice, before the day of reckoning.
- Review available visual aids; consider how these could and should be improved and by whom; then arrange for their creation in good time.
- Review your organisation's written promotional and presentational

material – from major, glossy brochures to, for example, quotations, tenders and estimates. If any fails to produce the correct image, replace it as soon as possible.

● Cost out your presentational efforts and compare them with, for example, the cost of producing estimates and products. If the balance is wrong, change it. If you need advice and help, take it.

This book is written to be read and, if possible, enjoyed. But it is also intended for re-reading and for reference. I hope that the ideas it produces will lead to the action you need, and that your pleasure in reading may turn to profit from action.

I wish you good fortune – in both senses of the word 'fortune' – luck and prosperity, through topping up your resources and your effort with the presentational skills they deserve.

Now – finally – some more checklists for your use.

72   Preparation

- What is the object of the exercise? How great are the winnings – as opposed to the resources that you will have to invest 'on spec'? Is the entire operation worth the time, effort and cost?
- If the answer is likely to be yes, then begin your preparations. These include consideration of each of the items listed in the checklists on pointers to success and to failure. Having done so, are you still satisfied that the gamble is worth your stake? If the answer is yes, decide:
  a) Which of your colleagues will you need, and how many, and at what level?
  b) Do you go to the prospects' premises? Or do you entice them to yours, so that they can 'inspect the company's facilities' – or be your guests for luncheon, after the presentation? Or do you meet on sensible, neutral ground?
- What *visual aids* should you prepare and use? Can your own resources or training department produce professional slides or transparencies, to reduce complicated figures or concepts to material with intelligent and precise impact? Or would it be better to prepare a set of vital documents for each of your audience?
- Are you satisfied that a *team* presentation will be just that – rather than a series of individual ones? Do all members of the team know their specific functions? Is each properly and fully briefed and prepared? Will they work together, sharing both the formal presentation and the (hopefully well-prepared) response to likely cross-examination?

Ask the four questions for winning in order:

- *Who* are your targets?
- *What* do *they* want from you?
- What is *your message*?
- *How* will you best put it across?

203

73   Positional checklist

When making your presentation, work out how best to station or position yourself. Consider:

- Should you sit or stand? Sitting is more informal and relaxed; standing more dominant. Much depends on the size and position of the audience; whether or not they can see you if seated; and your style.
- If you stand, should you move in front of the table, so as to remove the physical and atmospheric barrier between your audience and yourself? Moving up to the audience, if necessary detaching the microphone and taking it with you, is a highly professional and useful technique which creates a significant bond with the audience.
- If you are to stand for a protracted period, why not use a bar stool, draughtsman's chair or other high perch? If you sit or perch on the table, test it carefully – preferably beforehand. If it collapses under your weight or rolls away on castors, your presentation and your dignity will disappear at the same catastrophic moment.
- Stand or sit upright. Do not hunch forward or flop back into or onto a chair; or slouch, hands in pockets, on your platform.
- If you sit on a chair, stool or table in front of your audience, keep your legs together or crossed. You are not an advertisement for men's swimming trunks or women's underwear!
- To relax while sitting, try to get a 'carver' or chair with arms. Put it at an angle to the table, so that informality comes naturally.
- If you use visual aids, have you access to them? To trip/fall off the back or the front of the stage/knock down the easel – is a spectacular, non-recommended, but remarkably common phenomenon.
- Where and what is your amplification? Do you need a roving, portable microphone or other system which will give you freedom of movement? Otherwise, is your table or standing mike convenient to your preferred position and to your own height?
- Will you need a rostrum, or standing or table lectern?
- Never start your presentation until you have fully come to your feet – or until you have taken complete control of your audience, even if seated. Equally, do not sit down until you have finished talking and have nodded towards, or given a slight bow to, your audience. Indicate the same competence at the end of your presentation as your self-control showed at its start.
- Never turn your back on your audience. If you have to move across the room, whether to reach a visual aid or to speak to a member of your

audience or for whatever reason, keep your body facing your audience, or at least sideways.

- Straighten your tie, adjust your dress and brush the dandruff from your shoulders *before* you are called on to speak. Once the eyes of the audience are on you, these gestures are as undignified as the (equally common) scratching of the back, twiddling or clicking of the ball pen or unconscious cleaning of the ear.

- Get yourself into position – sitting or standing – and then wait until you have control of your audience, before you start speaking. If necessary and appropriate, tap on the table or on the side of a glass, with a coin or pencil. Wait until the Chair calls for and obtains orders. Far too many presenters actually begin their 'Ladies and Gentlemen' while in the process of rising to their feet.

- If you are nervous, write down your first words – even if it's only 'Ladies and Gentlemen' – and *always* write down any *names* that you may need to quote.

74   Success

What are the factors in a successful presentation? You are investing resources – time and its money's worth – in preparing and presenting your 'pitch'. So at least check to ensure that you are making the most of your opportunities.

- *Know your market.* Study and understand the motives of your potential clients or customers. Why are they prepared to spend time listening to you? What do they want and how can you provide it?
- *Marshal your contacts.* Find out through them how best to approach your audience – and your competition. Then consider how to handle each.
- *Create the right relationship with your audience.* As an interviewer, you know how much every interview depends upon personal intuition and judgment and how little on science. So if you can concoct the correct personal chemistry, you are well away.
- *Understand your audiences' needs.* Prime your commercial antennae to the needs-signals of your prospects – then respond to them.
- *Reputation matters* – yours and that of your prospects. If you have an established good name, build on it. If your reputation needs enhancing, use references – oral or written. Your prospects' reputations will guide you to their requirements.
- *The price must be right.* The value placed on your goods or services must be appropriate and correct. If the fee or cost is too high, you will price yourself out of the market. If your estimation of your own value is too low, then others may accept it, the result will be unprofitable, and you may even lose the contract to competitors who charge more.

  Presentation of price and value is as important as its assessment. Are you prepared to *explain and justify your charges?* Why, for instance, should your prospects pay more to you than to others? Conversely, if you are undercutting your competitors, then how can you manage to do so while preserving the excellence of your product or service?
- Are you sufficiently sensitive to your *prospects' problems?* Do you care enough about the job or the contact? Is your sensitivity apparent, so as to be convincing?
- Goods must be appropriately packaged for their market or they will not sell. So must services. Consider *who will present them* and *how?* Is an individual or team presentation appropriate? What documentation or visual aids should you supply? A worthwhile presentation is as carefully packaged as any product.
- Show that you *really want the job.* The three E's of presentation –

206

Enthusiasm, Energy and Excitement – are as essential as preparation, knowledge and understanding. Too many presentations collapse under the weight of apparent apathy.

- You must not only visibly and audibly want the job, but you must radiate *self-confidence* – confidence, that is, that you and your team and organisation are capable of doing it – well.
- *Be generous with your time* in providing initial explanations – especially of jargon or concepts that may be unfamiliar, if only to a few of your audience. If you lose them at the start, your message will be lost forever.
- *Open your mouth* and pronounce your words. Slovenly enunciation is like careless dress – discourteous and unacceptable.
- Say what you are going to say, say it, then say what you have said. *Repetition* is especially necessary where you have a complicated message to put over or a complex subject to teach.
- You must *talk your prospects' language* or they will not understand you. Take care to avoid your own jargon and where possible use theirs – but only with precision.
- If you are asked a question and do not know the answer, use one of the following tactics:
  1) *Say*: 'That's an interesting point, and if you will permit me, I shall deal with it shortly.' – then get one of your colleagues or associates to discover the answer for you. Or,
  2) *Say*: 'My colleague, Mr Jones, will be dealing with that important point very shortly.' Or,
  3) *Throw the question back to the enquirer*, thus: 'Thank you very much for that question – it is certainly an important one and we could research the answer for you. But perhaps you, sir, might be able to give us a guide to this territory. We know that your Mr White is extremely experienced in this area – and could have a word with our Mr Green, who could get together with him on it. They could also consider the problems of . . . and . . .' By now, you have already begun to deflect the questioner's interest and to change the subject. This could be dangerous, however, if you are dealing with a persistent, intelligent audience or a cunning adversary. Better to,
  4) *Admit that you do not know*, but say that you will find out. Make a note of the point to let them know that you really do intend to deal with it. Like an unexpected apology, this approach is refreshing and – providing that you are not dealing with an elementary point and that you do not use this approach too often – your honesty will be appreciated. When lecturing on complicated subjects – legal, commercial or political – I *always* prefer this tactic. Either I, or a colleague, will find out the answer – or sometimes someone in the audience will know it. Another example: 'Mr Jones, you have dealt with this sort of technical problem in your organisation. I wonder whether you could suggest the answer to Mr Gold's important question?'

75 Cardinal 'dont's'

For a checklist to *failure*, reverse the points made in the last chapter. Then add the following.

- Don't allow your team to *battle among themselves*. Never send a team of people who are obvious rivals. Their perceived conflict will soon convey itself to the purchasers. It is not only voters who shy away from a political party whose leaders do not agree – business people have the same reaction.
- Don't insist on making your presentation as you see fit without regard to your audience. If a questioner interrupts, tell him or her, politely, that question time comes at the end. *Inflexibility in approach* is an invitation to failure.
- Don't show your *prejudices*. Unpleasant jokes about Irish people or Jews, bias against women, hatred of trade unions will win you neither votes nor orders. The greater your prejudice, the greater the chance that your effort will be wasted.

Success depends on your own efforts – as compared with those of your competitors. If you are outsold; if your competitors follow my advice with greater care and alacrity than your colleagues and yourself – then they will win – especially if their prices are lower than yours.

The bigger and more successful your presentation, the more your prospects will feel that you consider their custom sufficiently important to warrant your maximum attention.

76 Changing minds and salvage operations

To make a presentation in expectation of success is difficult enough. Failure in the event becomes harder to bear.

Presentation in the teeth of assured failure is even more difficult. You have been tipped off that your prospects have decided against you? You are told, 'Well, it's pretty hopeless, but by all means talk to us, if you wish'? There are minds to change, tails to turn? Then check these tactical suggestions for presentations in the face of expected adversity. Pin-point the reason for your rejection – and, where possible, the individual responsible for it. Then concentrate your charm, your argument and your effort on:

- Weakening the arguments and the personal opposition ranged against you.
- Strengthening both your own case and those who may favour it.
- Looking for a warm and sympathetic response to a particular approach or argument and from an individual or minority, *however small* – blow on the sparks.
- Giving your opponents a line of dignified and sensible retreat. Be prepared to admit that an approach or argument may not be suitable for the needs, occasion or purpose – if that will enable your audience to accept another line, however little appeal it may previously have had to you.
- If your prospects seek to save face by blaming their previous rejection on some alleged failure on your part, accept the rebuke with good humour – provided only that it will not prejudice future confidence. With reasonable luck, perhaps tactfully assisted by you, all concerned will recognise the retreat for the intelligent and strategic withdrawal that it properly represents.
- If you cannot totally deflect your ill fortune, maybe you can keep a commercial foot in the customers' door? For instance, will they not give you at least a corner of the market? A share in the action?

77 Audience involvement

Your presentation cannot achieve its object unless your audience is involved. If its attention drifts, you are on the wrong course. Here are some top techniques for audience involvement:

- After your opening greetings and ice-breaking remarks, immediately question your audience, asking, for example: 'Where do you come from?'; 'What is your particular interest in this subject?'; 'Have you had particular problems in this area, sir?'; 'Madam, can we start by focusing on your specific interest in this presentation?' Or simply: 'How many of you said to your wives and husbands, "What a boring morning I've got today . . . a presentation on . . ."'? Well, it's not going to be like that, I want to show you the vast fascination, importance and potential profitability of . . .'
- Ask questions, but beware of the rhetorical. If skilfully used, a rhetorical question is a powerful weapon. If misused, it backfires. In general, a rhetorical question should only be asked if you do not care whether or not you get an answer – and if that answer is the wrong one, then you should be able to deflect with laughter. 'We all agree, don't we?' – watch out for the rumbled, grumbled 'Certainly not'. Pounce on the interrupter – 'We have a dissident. Tell me, sir, why do you disagree?'
- At the end of each theme – especially if you are dealing with complicated material – ask: 'Is that clear?' Or: 'Mr Brown – you are particularly involved in this area. Have I covered the points you wanted or would you like to ask any questions?'
- Involve the senior, most distinguished and powerful listeners. 'Ms Green – you are Marketing Director and responsible for this territory. Would you care to comment on this theme and perhaps add to it?'
- If the audience gets restless, has the time come to give it (literally) a rest? To pause for refreshment, perhaps? With a large audience, a complicated subject and a friendly atmosphere, I sometimes require my audience to stand up, stretch their arms upwards and try to touch the ceiling – which leads to inevitable hilarity and simulated complaint. 'Come on, you at the back! Stand up and stretch – it will do a power of good to your alleged minds to give your bodies rare exercise!'
- Invite questions – but do not be put off by a long pause before the first response. This is normal. But if it continues too long, pick on an individual. 'Mr White, what do you think?' 'Mr Gold, what would you like to know that I haven't dealt with?'
- If your audience is large or at a distance, do not be afraid to move in and

among them (see positional checklist in Chapter 73). Watch how skilled cabaret artists operate, and copy them.

- Keep eye contact with your audience. Watch them with hawk-like intent. If attention wanders, focus on the inattention.
- Show your interest in each person in your audience. If the audience is small, then look from person to person. If it is large, try to keep each person alert, wondering when you are next going to pick on him or her.
- Use interruptions to flavour your talk. The passing aircraft; the invading tea trolley; the delegate who wanders in late ('Good evening, sir. We are just finishing.' – this, of course, in the morning and just after the presentation has begun) – each can provide a peg for comment or wit. But never let an interruption disturb *you*.
- Every skilled political speaker welcomes hecklers. They bring the audience to life; to its feet; and onto his or her side. So do not despise the unfriendly interruption – use it.
- Never fear to vary your style, content or approach if your audience is unimpressed or switching off. Use stories and humour to flavour your presentation. Conversely, if a humorous presentation (perhaps in an after-dinner speech) is leaving your audience cold, warm them up on some serious content. Always remember your presentation is for the benefit of others and if you cannot get and keep them involved, you are better off to switch off, move off, and go home.
- Remember with kindness those who may not wish to ask questions because they are afraid of appearing foolish – perhaps through not understanding jargon with which they feel that they should be familiar.
- Pick up ideas from your audience and write them on your flip chart. 'Let's just jot down, shall we, the various markets (or as the case may be)?'

78   On paper

Appearances count – personal, when in person or on TV; oral, aural and vocal on radio. But in the absence of sight or sound, you will be judged on paper. So here is a basic checklist for paper presentations.

The paper itself

Choose your paper with care. Check:

- *Quality* – including thickness, feel and appearance.
- *Cost* – in relation to both purpose and quantity. Do you wish to impress by style and prestige – or will too fine a quality or too smart an appearance indicate an over-expensive product?
- *Use* – If you are intending to photocopy from a 'master' sheet onto the presentation paper, make sure your photographer can cope with the weight of paper you are ordering. If it is too heavy or thick it will simply jam in the machine, and you will be left with a broken copier and an expensive pile of scrap paper.

Headings, logos and printing

Choose with care your style of heading and of printing. Select a logo which will be striking, memorable and appropriate. Balance the size and placing of the print – on the top and/or the bottom of the page.

You may need help from a professional designer or commercial artist. Or you may get equally good results from a first-class and experienced printer – especially one who knows your own style and approach.

Proofs

Insist that you get proofs, and that they arrive in good time to make any necessary changes. These changes should be kept to a minimum because they involve expense for the printer which (dependent upon the contract and/or goodwill of the printer or designer) may be passed on (in whole or in part) to you.

Proof-reading requires immaculate care. Amazing misspellings escape the proof-reader's eye – and once you have had, and approved the proofs, you can no longer blame the printer if the paper has to be scrapped.

Also, check carefully the following:

- The relationship between the print (including the varying sizes), the logo and the paper.
- The size of specific lines, for example you will not want 'From the Managing Director' (or as the case may be) too large.
- Ensure that the logo is precisely upright – and, if appropriate, in line and squared up with the paper itself and/or other printing on it.

Colour and embossing

One colour is cheaper than two; simple printing less costly than embossed or other raised type. However, once the printer has prepared your dye, block or other special equipment requirement, actual printing costs should be unaffected – both on the initial printing and later.

Carefully select the colour or colours of: a) the paper itself, and b) the print. Starting with the basic black print on white paper, there are almost endless variations. If you find one that suits you and your product particularly well, you may wish to make it into a 'house colour' – immediately identifiable by (at least regular) recipients, and conveying the intended impression of your product, your services or yourself.

Cost

Unless you are a bulk buyer, the purchase of the paper itself will depend little on quantity. But it is invariably cheaper to *print* in quantity. Typesetting, preparation of machinery, and the general cost benefits of large-scale production all militate towards increase of cost for small quantities and reduction for scale.

However, the larger the scale, the smaller the reduction created in the price – so check whether you may need to change the paper because:

- The individuals whose names appear on it may move;
- Addresses, telephone numbers, fax or telex details may be altered; or
- You may tire, or think better, of the design, logo, etc.

Get quotes. The cost of the paper itself and of the printing on it may vary dramatically.

Time

Use this checklist early. Give yourself time to make your choices, obtain your quotations, increase your options, vary your requirements, and consult your colleagues or experts. Give your designers and printers time to do the job properly so that you do not have to pay a premium for a rush job. A good written presentation is well worth the paper on which it is printed.

(For more on written presentations, see *Janner's Complete Letterwriter*.)

79 Venue

Too often, presenters have their venues thrust upon them. The meeting, the organisational gathering or the dinner party is held in a place selected by others. Even there, though, foresight and skill may help you make the best of your surroundings.

Sometimes, you can influence, if not choose, the venue for your presentation. What should you look for?

First, try to match the size of the room to the number in the audience. Pack them in. Take fifty and squeeze them into a small room and you should have a lively, useful meeting. Lose those same fifty in a hall and the event is a failure before it begins. So underestimate your expected audience. If some stand or a few get left outside, never mind. Next time they will come earlier. Avoid the echoing emptiness of a half-filled hall.

If your audience is sparse, do not panic. Ask everyone to come up to the front. Most people hate being up front. They prefer to tuck themselves away into a nook near the door, the better to doze or to exit if they get bored. But a capable Chair or speaker can wheedle most people into helping by saying, for example, 'Please do gather round.'

Sometimes, it is better to abandon the platform, draw the curtains on the stage, then descend into your audience. At least ensure that your chat is informal, so that your audience feel that they have made personal contact with the speaker. Ignore the numbers and present the same oration to an almost empty room as you would to a packed and cheering hall and you are compounding the error of those who overestimate the audience.

If the room is too hot, stop and ask for a window or a door to be opened. Your audience will bless you. Or if the place is freezing, speak to the organisers. Even if nothing can be done, your audience will know that you are thinking of their comfort.

If aircraft pass overhead, pause. To ramble on, irrespective of the row, is a sure sign of inexperience. If a carpenter is banging next door or a pneumatic drill shatters the road and its silence, ask the Chair to use influence to douse the noise.

It is better, of course, to deal with distractions in advance. Get to a meeting early; induce the organisers to re-arrange the seating to suit your theme or your plans. Do you wish to use a platform or have the chairs arranged informally in a horseshoe? If the audience may be small, why not close off the balcony and rope off part of the downstairs area until the centre is filled?

Do get the sound equipment tested and the lighting adjusted before the audience arrives. To make your preparations after your guests appear is inefficient and discourteous.

If you wish to make a triumphal entry at a later stage, you can always disappear from the scene until the mighty moment. If your hosts know their business, they will have organised a small room at the back for you to use for your coat, your hat, your refreshment – and your disappearing act. To rise to the occasion, you must prepare your venue, as well as yourself.

Finally, a few more points you should always consider before the event:

- How are you going to separate smokers from the non-smokers? Smokers to the back? Or to one side? Or perhaps you should prohibit smoking altogether?
- If you expect your delegates or audience to make notes, are they seated at desks or tables and have you provided them with pens, pencils and pads?
- Do you want people to be identified by lapel badges or by name cards placed in front of them?
- If you are going to invite questions from your audience, are enough roving microphones available so that the audience can hear the questions as well as the answers?
- What arrangements have been made to receive people at the start of the day? Try to ensure that the reception/coffee area is entirely separate from the lecture room, so that people do not wander in and around while the equipment is being sorted and set up. This way you will also avoid the clatter of crockery and cutlery before and after the coffee breaks.
- If your presentation is in the form of a lecture at a conference or seminar, have you arranged for appropriate documentation to be available in the lecture room? When and how will it be distributed? Clear, well-presented and comprehensive documentation reflects the professionalism of the speaker and the conference organisers. Remember also that the documentation may be the only tangible thing that delegates take away with them – a permanent reminder of an enjoyable and successful day!

80   Get trained

You may learn microphone techniques and all the other essentials of presentation through trial and error. The errors will be yours; the trials imposed on others, and the chances of your doing justice to yourself and to your company or firm are far less than your prospects of losing your position. The alternative is – training.

Does your company employ training officers to look after such recognised essentials as induction training of recruits and teaching craftsmen and others the skills necessary to increase productivity? The idea that managers should themselves submit to training – especially in anything that until recently has been self-taught, like presentational skills – is abhorrent. Or is it? Colleagues and I have taught these skills to some of Britain's top business and professional people. For many, this training is top secret. It is carried out in privacy, with our own staff operating that invaluable audio visual equipment and without any of his or her colleagues knowing.

More often, we take groups of between two and six people, usually of the same standing, and prepared (if necessary) to laugh at themselves and to put up with embarrassment in the good cause of swift learning. We usually teach in pairs, one of whom is always a specialist in voice production and projection.

We believe that the top training method is to submit those whose presentations are crucial to their business to individual teaching and practice, under skilled and independent eyes – and to submit them to affectionate criticism from those who could have no interest other than their success.

Methods must vary according to needs and people. There are, though, a number of constants:

- At less senior levels, we take larger numbers, or one trainer will teach up to eight people.
- The video camera, playback TV screen and other closed circuit apparatus are essential. Delegates learn more from watching themselves than anyone could teach them.
- Victims criticise each other – and themselves. That criticism is – with no exception in our experience – constructive. It is also frank, and itself subject to criticism by us.

- The principles explained in this book must be learned – from preparation through the use of visual aids, to the presentational skills themselves and never forgetting the message, the proposal, the object of each exercise and how to maximise prospects of attaining it.
- Wherever possible, the sessions are spread over two days. Somehow, sleeping on the first day's lessons imprints them on the mind and turns them into action.

Following these methods and using the impact of independent and personalised criticism will bring results rapidly, and often dramatically. We have seen shy delegates learn to dominate vast meetings; self-effacing and brilliant technicians find they can make witty after-dinner speeches; and unwilling speakers discover the arts of chairing turbulent meetings or presenting complicated proposals with confidence and craft. Fine speakers can become even more expert.

The object of presentational training should be to enable the individual to put across his or her own particular talent, with personal style and stylish personality. Naturally, this involves an investment in time and resources. But if it does not provide value for money, then you have not chosen the best trainers and methods for your needs.

So, study, absorb and use the techniques, explained in this book. Train and practise, and accept the fun and the challenge of fine presentational skills. You will deserve to succeed – and you will. Good luck!

Index

deflecting 150–2, 207
    rhetorical 210
    use for audience involvement 210
quotations, use of 51–2

racism 20
radio interviews 121–30
    anecdotes in 127
    phone-ins 128–30
    preparation for 121–2
    scripts for 123
    style in 124–6
reading
    as training for writing 68, 69
    in presentations 53–4
Reagan, Ronald 124
reception/reception area 216
references 89, 196–7
registration of voters 193
rehearsals, television 135–6
relaxed interviews/presentations 55,
    126
repetition 207
reputation 206
resignation, threats of 80
resources, and elections 194
restlessness/boredom in audience
    16, 17, 34, 187, 211
'rules of order' 77

sailing 76
salaries 28, 152
sales cassettes 46
sales conferences 91
sales staff 27, 91
schools 69
scientists 4
scripts
    for presentations 53–4, 55–6
    for radio 123
seating 97, 99, 215–16
self-confidence *see* confidence
self-control 143
self-interest in charity 103–4
self-presentation
    and appearance 8–9
    and body language 10–11
    and flattery 14–15
    and humour 20–2

and nervousness 12–13, 63
    and pauses 14–15
    and sensitivity 16–18, 26–7
    and use of language 30–1
    education/training in 6–7
    importance of 3–5
    style of 6, 7
selling, presentations for 87–106
    close-up 101–2
    conferences/seminars 96–7
    fund-raising 103–5
    launches 94–5
    meals/banquets 98–100
    proposals for 89
    sales conferences 91
    tactics for 87–8
    tenders/estimates 92–3
selling teams 82
sensitivity 16–18, 26–7, 206
sentences 70
Shakespeare, William 7, 69
Shaw, Bernard 69
Shinwell, Lord 'Manny' 64, 80
shop stewards 27–8
silence, use of 14, 15
sincerity, appearance of 25, 125–6
sitting 11, 13, 204
size of rooms for presentations 99,
    190, 215
slander 195
slides 41–2, 43, 44, 45
smoking 97, 216
Soviet Union 175
Speakers' Corner 190
speechwriters 54
split infinitives 71
sponsorship 163
Stalin, Josef 33
standing 10, 204
stationery/paper 212–14
statistics, use of 52
Stevenson, Adlai 35
stills, series of 49
stories 20, 23, 66, 127, 186–7, 211
stress 12, 26
style
    in letterwriting 68–71
    in radio interviews 124–6
    of articles 162